# FORMER STUDENTS TALK ABOUT THIS BOOK

"Dr. Weber's 6 step approach was a great help to me in exploring and ultimately determining my primary interests in the broad field of marketing, and then systematically pursuing a path that led me to the first step in my career with Google. After assembling my resume and stories to tell about my leadership and relevant experiences, I found a sponsor at Google, who advocated for me to interview. Dr. Weber's interview strategies and tips made me feel confident going into my interviews. I can credit this confidence for successfully making it through the interviewing process and ultimately receiving my offer! This 6 step system is a great formula for identifying one's strengths and finding a way to make your first job a reality!"

**Katie Menzner**
*Account Manager, Google*

"Using this process helped me greatly in landing my position with Clarion Market Research. I think the most important and valuable component of the approach for me was learning how to develop and use my specifically focused 'Leadership Stories.' I designed each story to highlight how my skills and experiences demonstrated my ability to complete the job requirements that were being sought. This enhanced my applications, moving me on to the interview process. In the interviews themselves, my stories made me feel prepared and confident, and helped to make my interviews enthusiastic, credible and less rehearsed – ultimately landing me my dream starting position in marketing research."

**Karina Rappaccioli**
*Assistant Project Director, Clarion Market Research*

"This process really works! I received an offer for my dream entry-level position a week after graduating, and I owe it all to these six steps. Finding an internal sponsor was crucial to developing a better understanding of the company and role that I was applying for. This also allowed me to add an employee reference to my application, which helped my resume to stand out in the thousands that were received. I was able to navigate the proceeding interviews with the help of my sponsor and the interview strategies provided in this book. I would highly recommend this process to all marketing students hoping to enter the workforce after their undergraduate career!"

**Allison Kerins**
*Sales Representative, MillerCoors*

"By using this systematic approach, I had an actionable timeline for pursing the broad and seemingly overwhelming task of finding my first marketing position. The results-focused framework presented in this book really helped me understand the key steps and strategies in landing a dream job. At the start of my search, it was important to learn about the various marketing job opportunities available to me. I then narrowed my search to positions that matched my values, interests and career development plan. After completing more research, I tailored my resume, cover letter and interview stories to these specific opportunities. Career advisers, teachers and mentors provided great feedback and support throughout the process. I worked to be as authentic as ⸻ ⸻ asked many questions tailored to the specific oppor⸻ ⸻ ⸻als in the organization. I highly recommend utilizir⸻ ⸻, enjoy the process, and find the best opportunity to la⸻

**e McGuire**
*rchandising*

D1306076

"For me, three focal points of Professor Weber's process helped me the most in landing my dream job right out of college. These included sorting out my interests, documenting my experiences and then building and using my network. As you begin, you are asked and helped to search out an area of marketing that is of strongest personal interest to you. Next comes help to identify and then describe your relevant skills and experiences for your targeted position, both on your resume and in person in your "leadership stories" (a particularly strong point of emphasis and relevance in the process detailed in this book). Finally, having a strong endorsement from a knowledgeable and trusted person within the field – i.e., a "sponsor" in the book's terminology – will help you immensely in guiding you through the interview maze to an attractive offer. This process works and I highly recommend it for anyone trying to launch a career in marketing!"

**Jennifer Teshima**
*Master Data Administrator, Manitowoc Foodservice*

"By carefully following the process described in this book, I landed my dream job straight out of college. The first steps to identify and then find your dream target position(s) require considerable time and thought, but the guidelines provided help to ease that process. After that, using the step-by step networking and the interviewing tips clearly outlined in the book gave me the confidence to relax and be myself while pursuing a job. In fact, I even learned to enjoy "networking," a word and process that used to make me cringe."

**Meg Vonderhaar**
*Designer, Big Tomorrow Design Corp., Austin, TX*

"Being exposed to Professor Weber's systematic approach was a game changer in getting my career started. One of the most difficult aspects of my search was figuring out exactly what I wanted to do. This approach helped me to do just this and also enabled me to stand out among my peers during the search and interview process. Getting that first job coming right out of college with very little experience is challenging for anyone. For me personally, using the process presented in this book enabled me to confidently and successfully tackle that challenge head on."

**Kyle Rubbinaccio**
*Market Analyst at Morgan Stanley*

"Following the six step approach presented in this book was a tremendous help in getting my career started. It made me think back to what attracted me to marketing in the first place and to what areas of marketing turned out to be of most personal interest. Having a systematic process stimulated me to tackle the 'get a job' challenge head on. It gave me specific tips for pulling from my course learning and my internship to enhance my resume, my stories and my interview skills. The book emphasizes and clarifies how the job search process goes so much further than simply submitting one's resume online and hoping for the best. The process helped me to get all my materials and background together, and search for relevant potential opportunities. The key turning point for me was getting a sponsor who helped guide me, along with my resume, through the interviewing maze and up to the top of the resume stack. That was crucial for me as it got me the opportunity to use the interview tips in the book to tell my stories confidently and enthusiastically, which I am convinced eventually got me the job offer. Overall, I am a huge fan of the process, as my personal experience confirmed that following this approach can put anyone on the path for successfully taking that first step in your career: getting that first job!"

**Rachel Nestor**
*Inventory Planning, Dick's Sporting Goods*

# Land Your Dream Job in Marketing

"The six-step approach developed by Professor Weber and used by many of us at Notre Dame really forced me to dig deep on multiple levels. First, I had to think about what I would enjoy doing and what I believed I was good at. Then, I had to find a match by analyzing what specific available jobs attracted me and matched both my hard and soft skills. I needed to objectively sort out my skills to identify the right possible positions and carefully study the descriptions and responsibilities of specific available jobs to try to find the best match between my skills and the companies' needs. Then, prior to approaching any company, I had to reflect on my own previous experiences, no matter how big or small, and to craft them into engaging stories that highlight the skills my target employers were looking for. A simple "Yes, I can do that" does not fly in the job market; I needed to be able to be able to say, "Yes, I have done that" **and** follow up with a compelling story to really make headway in the interview room. Overall, learning and implementing the holistic approach presented in this book is a challenging and powerful experience that can put anyone at a strategic advantage. This both helps and stimulates recruiters and others influential in the hiring process to vault you, with your relevant experiences, to the top of the resume stack."

**Chris Jacques**
*Account Manager at Braintree (PayPal & Venmo)*

"The six-step approach developed by Professor Weber was critical for me in landing my dream job in marketing. When I first started applying for jobs, I submitted my resume to anyone that would take it. They weren't necessarily the right jobs nor did they have descriptions that met my skill set. After taking a step back and focusing on these strategic six steps, I could walk into interviews confident in my ability to answer any question about my qualifications for the job at hand because I had identified the positions that matched my qualifications. As part of giving me an overall job search plan, I think my biggest personal takeaway was how it stimulated me to build my leadership stories to support what I felt were and are my strongest qualifications. More and more employers are looking for much more than a statement that you have a certain skill and related background. They want relevant examples of how you have demonstrated those specific skills and that is where my stories really made the difference for me. Having these stories at the ready to supplement my resume set me apart from the applicant pool and ultimately landed me the job I love today. "

**Christine Wuertz**
*Implementation Manager, Digital Marketing, Sims Partners*

"I remember thinking, as a senior at Notre Dame, how overwhelmed I was with wanting to explore and consider so many marketing job possibilities. I didn't want to make a bad decision or choose the wrong path to start my career. Looking back, there wouldn't have been a wrong choice. Every single job you have, even if it's not THE perfect job, is a learning experience that leads you to ultimately finding and landing that dream role. As this book details, it's all about knowing yourself and your strengths and then selling those on your resume, cover letter and, most importantly, through your networking and interviewing. Be confident, be determined, stay positive and you will land where you are meant to be!"

**Kristen Stoutenburgh**
*Digital Marketing, American Airlines*

# How to Land Your Dream Job in Marketing
## 6 steps to finding and winning your first marketing position

Dr. John A. Weber, University of Notre Dame
Kate Ferrara, Nielsen Corp.

# How to Land Your Dream Job in Marketing
## 6 steps to finding and winning your first marketing position

ISBN-10: 0-9895006-7-5
ISBN-13: 978-0-9895006-7-8

Printed by CreateSpace

Author Contact Information
Dr. John A. Weber
Weber.1@nd.edu
Mendoza College of Business
University of Notre Dame
Notre Dame, In 46556

**Cover Design** by Meg Vonderhaar
**Editing** by Lesley Stevenson and Kayla Mullen

**Dedication**

For all present and future marketing students – wishing you the best in your search for that elusive dream job in marketing

# INTRODUCTION & OVERVIEW

*"Despite the seemingly endless stresses and decisions made during college, none are quite as daunting as making that first leap into a career. Especially with marketing, where there isn't a "track" or a "Big 4" equivalent, finding a fulfilling, well-paying and interesting job can be a challenge. Fortunately for students interested in Marketing, Professor Weber's years of assisting students to land jobs are an invaluable resource. How to Land Your Dream Job in Marketing has distilled all of that knowledge into 6 steps to help aspiring marketers find and land that dream job."*

**Kevin Moyer**

*Recent graduate, now Solutions Engineering Consultant, Salesforce.com*

A near half-century career here at the University of Notre Dame has provided the opportunity to work with many thousands of undergraduate marketing students. Nothing is more satisfying than to have the opportunity to help some of them land that first job, and to help many of them again later on, as they seek to transition that first position into a long and satisfying marketing career.

Through consultations with recruiters and former students, through testing recommendations of many professional career coaches, and through active trial and error with different techniques and approaches, we have developed a series of 6 steps – a systematic process—that many students have found useful in their search for that first, entry-level marketing job, *and* for advancing their careers in marketing over time.

Few students have actually used all 6 steps. That said, virtually all students who have sought help have found that the content of at least one of these steps has aided them significantly in the effort to find and capture that oft-times elusive first marketing position.

The book offers suggestions for young marketing professionals, as well. In recent years, a seemingly larger and larger proportion of those seeking career assistance are young folks who graduated one to three years ago. They are now looking for continuing counsel and advice to move their careers forward – frequently altering the original direction of their career paths. They too have found the overall process – or at least particular components of the process – to be very helpful.

# OVERVIEW – OUTLINE

**The six step systematic approach** is designed to help graduating marketing students find and capture more attractive entry-level marketing positions.

1. **What Is Your Dream Marketing Job?** Step 1 is to review and help the student decide which area of marketing seems best for that student, given that student's specific preferences, background and qualifications.

2. **Prepare Your Materials for Your Search.** Step 2 is to help refine the student's resume and to provide suggestions and guidance for building "leadership stories" that the student can subsequently use in all communications and interviews with recruiters to showcase the student's relevant background and experiences.

3. **Searching for and Finding Relevant Opportunities.** Step 3 is to help the student search out and find specific alternative available job (and internship) opportunities that match that student's specific preferences, background and qualifications.

4. **Application Strategies and Tips.** Step 4 focuses on finding and using an internal company sponsor at any relevant target company. Through that sponsor, the student then submits his or her credentials, cover letter, and application, thereby getting closer consideration and hopefully getting express treatment right on to the "short stack" of candidates.

5. **Interview Strategies and Tips.** Step 5 is to provide a series of strategies and tips for interviews that have been garnered and consolidated from a wide variety of recruiters, hiring managers, career counselors and the authors' own experiences.

6. **Evaluating and Negotiating an Offer.** Step 6 is to provide the student with perspectives, general advice and counsel on offers received, including negotiation advice if and when it seems appropriate.

## ACKNOWLEDGEMENTS

As mentioned in the introduction, much of the specific content of the individual steps in the process presented in this book flows from creative ideas of recruiters and professional career counselors. Without mentioning specific names for fear of slighting anyone who has contributed directly or indirectly, the list of those contributing most to this book – either directly, or indirectly – includes incredibly insightful recruiters from companies such as Google, IBM, Target, General Mills, Starcom MediaVest, Nielsen, AT&T, Gallo, LinkedIn and many others. We have also gleaned many ideas from career coaches at Careercast.com, Aboutmoney.com, Marketingabout.com, Indeed.com, Jeff-the-careercoach.com, LinkedIn.com, Themuse.com, Outspokenmedia.com, Simplyhired.com, aiesec.com Exploremarketingcareers-.com, Roberthalf.com, Collegerecruiter.com, Quintessential.com, Quint-careers.com, Glassdoor.com, Wired.com and Work.chron.com. Ideas from author Eric Siebert (Careers in Marketing, 2016), and folks at Career Centers at the University of Notre Dame, University of Vermont, and University of California, Santa Cruz have also been most influential. Thanks to all for your direct or indirect contributions.

We enthusiastically acknowledge and thank Meg Vonderhaar for her cover and jacket design and both Lesley Stevenson and Kayla Mullen for their astute editorial work, with additional assistance from Maggie Weber.

# CONTENTS

## Step 5 - Interview Strategies and Tips

## Step 6 - Evaluating and Negotiating Your Offer

# STEP 1
## WHAT IS YOUR DREAM MARKETING JOB?

## QUICK START

Marketing is a field brimming with all kinds of exciting and stimulating jobs. Consider the range of possibilities below. Challenging, lucrative career opportunities exist in each of these areas—it all depends on what you want to do!

# WHERE TO START?

So what is your dream entry-level job? Explore each area in the diagram above and identify one or two general areas you feel best match your interests and skills.

This chapter will help you by explaining the day-to-day responsibilities and requirements of each area. We've included examples of actual 23- to 24 year-old professionals working entry-level positions to give you a better feel for each area.

The general marketing area (or areas) that you choose to pursue does not necessarily have to match your background to date, as long as you have a strong interest and aptitude in that area. You're young and, as long as you have the skills required for an area, with a concerted effort and solid training, you can quickly build the background to succeed in almost any marketing area of interest. We elaborate upon this point later in Step 2—note the difference between background and aptitudes.

## YOUR DREAM MARKETING JOB IS DYNAMIC

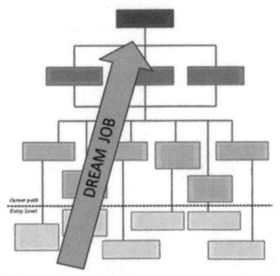

Regardless of which general area of marketing you pursue, the nature of your dream job will shift over time. Step 1 will help you envision an imaginary line between top management career positions and entry-level positions in each area. As expected, no one starts at the top.

For example, consider positions in an advertising agency. Your dream entry-level job might be as a media planner or digital advertising analyst. During the first couple of years, you gain valuable experience and, assuming you demonstrate commitment and a quality performance, you quickly move up the organizational structure. As that happens, your dream marketing job will likely transition to account executive for a small client or assistant account executive for a major client and so on, over time.

Meanwhile, your opportunities for learning and compensation increase along with your responsibilities.

Over time—much less time than most new marketers expect—what you regard as your dream marketing job will continue to move upward every year or two in breadth and depth of responsibility. You and your dream marketing position can climb as fast and high as your energy, talent, and commitment will take you.

As your experience and network grow, new opportunities outside your original company will also arise. Former colleagues who have moved to other companies will contact and recommend you as attractive new positions open. Headhunters will also seek you out as your resume and portfolio of experience and accomplishments expand. In sum, new opportunities will arise regularly. So too, your dream marketing position will continually change over time.

## WHICH AREA IS RIGHT FOR YOU?

The field of marketing is diverse, fun, challenging, and competitive and offers great rewards to those with the energy, ambition, and work ethic to succeed.[1]

# STARTING YOUR SEARCH[2]

Begin by considering these points that will help you frame and filter your exploration for meaningful and satisfying entry-level marketing positions—both full-time and internship options.

## WHAT INTERESTS YOU?

### Which positions most interest you?

Consider some of the most popular marketing careers available, such as those in:

- ❖ Sales and sales management—consumer or business to business products and services
- ❖ Public relations
- ❖ Retail—analysis and planning at corporate level or in-store retail sales, merchandising, or store management
- ❖ Market data analytics and market research
- ❖ Digital, interactive and social media marketing
- ❖ Brand and product management
- ❖ Advertising and promotion (e.g., strategy, media planning, creative direction, and graphic design)

❖ And many others (specific examples appear below)

Which area or areas excite you the most? Where do your interests, experiences, and aspirations best fit? We suggest you review the examples of various entry-level marketing positions below, just to see if any spark an initial interest. There are, of course, dozens of other possibilities as well, but these descriptive examples should help you get started in your exploration for something right for you.

## What type of company interests you?

❖ Do you have a preference for working in a particular industry?
❖ In a particular location?
❖ For a company with a particular type of culture and work-life balance?
❖ How about the size of company? Would you prefer to work for small or medium-sized businesses or a larger, more well-known corporation?
❖ How about working in marketing for a not-for-profit entity?

## Consider other potential limiting factors.

❖ Do you want to look only for full-time jobs?
❖ Is an internship with the prospect of full-time offer at the end acceptable?
❖ Is a rotational training program required? Is this problematic?
❖ What is the minimum salary you will accept?
❖ What is the maximum number of hours you want to work in a week?
❖ What is the minimum paid time off you will accept?
❖ What is the minimum signing bonus and/or moving expenses you want?
❖ Do you have other limitations or preferences?

Your answers to these initial questions will help you to focus your search for a relevant and attractive entry-level position.

# INITIAL CLARIFICATIONS

## Marketing opportunities are open to college grads with nearly any background.[3]

While many marketing professionals hold a post-secondary degree in marketing, many don't. For the past few decades, modes of communication have been changing drastically, from paper and television to online and mobile. Correspondingly, marketing requires taking an innovative spin to suit the needs of consumers. The pace of change easily surpasses the integration between academia and applicability. In other words, what you learn about marketing in a formal school setting could be helpful; however, it is not enough to secure your success as a marketer. This is why the marketing industry invites talents from all educational backgrounds, not simply those who hold a marketing degree.

For marketing, sales, and management, perhaps those with a degree in business administration or marketing are more suitable. When it comes to marketing for highly technical industries, those with an engineering background certainly have an advantage. According to a survey done on digital marketers, only one-third of respondents had a business and marketing degree; the rest studied computer science, humanities, social sciences, or even criminal justice. Likewise, only 9 percent of respondents said they had taken courses specifically in digital marketing—the lack of education did not prevent the other 91 percent from reaching success. Many respondents pointed out that you can learn marketing from trying and doing, instead of from the books.

Marketing essentially builds on communication and promotion, and the skills required are highly transferable from other educational disciplines or even life experiences. Have you ever thought that studying a foreign language or having a multicultural experience could enhance your chances of being a successful marketer? Marketing demands an ability to adapt, to understand your own and others' strengths and weaknesses, and to have passion and expertise. Employers are willing to hire anyone who demonstrates these qualities.

# There's a difference between advertising and marketing[4]

Many confuse advertising with marketing. Start with the formal definitions:

* ❖ *Advertising:* A component of marketing, advertising is the paid, public, non-personal announcement of a persuasive message by an identified sponsor; the non-personal presentation or promotion by a firm of its products or services to a company's existing and potential customers.
* ❖ *Marketing:* Think of marketing as everything that an organization does to facilitate an exchange between company and consumer. This includes systematically planning, implementing, and controlling a mix of business activities intended to bring together buyers and sellers for the mutually advantageous exchange or transfer of products or services.

To clarify, advertising is a single component of the overall marketing process. Mainstream marketers (e.g., product and brand managers) determine the overall design of marketing programs (market research, target segment selection, key competitive differentiators, price points, distribution, sales strategies, customer support, and the desired focus of messaging to selected target segments).

Advertisers (in house or agencies) develop and then deliver the desired messaging to the target segments. This includes developing and implementing ad design for different media (e.g., print, digital, broadcast, etc.), media placement and timing, and the measurement of results. Thus, advertising essentially involves getting the word out and planning growth strategies for a company's products and services. Advertising tends to be the largest marketing expense category for many companies—particularly for companies selling primarily to final consumer markets as opposed to those selling to business customers.

Another way to distinguish between advertising and marketing is to think of marketing as a pie. Inside that pie, you have slices of advertising, market research, public relations, product pricing, distribution, customer support, sales strategy, and community involvement. Advertising only equals one piece of the pie in the company's overall set of strategies. While these different marketing components work independently, it is the responsibility of marketing management (e.g., market, product, and brand managers) to ensure that all these components work together towards the bigger goal.

# Three things you might not want to hear:

* Advertising is a super competitive field, is difficult to break into, and provides comparatively low starting salaries.
* Some sales background is critical if your ultimate desire is to become a mainstream brand, product, or marketing manager.
* Successful sports marketing careers are rare—beware. In the following section, we consider each of these points.

## Entry-level positions in advertising are hard to get.

A large proportion of marketing students favor would-be jobs in advertising. If this includes you, then you should be overtly aware of several important factors.

* ***Competition***: Advertising is extremely competitive. Dozens of candidates vie for each position. Successful candidates have strong resumes, robust portfolios, and refined communication and interview skills.
* ***Internships as a first step***: Initial positions in advertising are often internships, even for college graduates. Superior performance in an internship often leads to a full time offer, but it is not guaranteed.
* ***Late offers and dynamic agency needs***: Many, if not most, advertising positions don't become available until spring—even late spring—of senior year. Many advertising agencies hire to fill manpower needs for servicing specific clients, and each agency's client base tends to ebb and flow. Thus, each agency's manpower needs are in flux.
* ***Low starting salaries***. The starting salary for some entry-level ad agency positions (e.g., media planning) is typically significantly lower (e.g., 40 percent lower) than for more mainstream marketing positions.
* ***Salaries catch up later***. On the other hand, the first promotion in such positions can yield raises of 50 percent or more, with ultimate salaries matching or at least coming close to the typical salaries for other mainstream marketing positions.

## Sales is the best entry point for most brand, product, or general marketing manager positions.

Many marketing students favor would-be entry-level positions in brand, product, or general marketing management while eschewing entry-level positions in sales. If that includes you, then give the following points careful consideration.

* *Brand, product, and general marketing managers must have experience.* To even receive consideration for one of these positions, most companies require that any potentially viable candidate has thorough knowledge of the company's relevant market solutions (products and services) and various target customer segments.

* *A sales background will help you*. How do you best get that knowledge? Through selling. If you really aspire to a mainstream marketing position in a known company, suck it up. Start in sales. Become a sales superstar. In most companies, that will give you the credentials to be realistically considered for a mainstream marketing position after a few years.

* *We are not suggesting sales positions for used car dealerships, vacuum cleaners, makeup, or multi-level/pyramid scheme sales.* We are suggesting respected professional selling positions for highly regarded consumer goods and business-to-business solution providers—these positions can be challenging, stimulating, and personally and financially rewarding. Often, they're also more related to your marketing degree than you might think. On top of that, starting salaries for salesmen can be quite competitive, with the higher end reaching up to $150,000 or more!

* *Echoing the above—you have to pay your dues.* "You have to earn a job in mainstream marketing (brand, product and market management), and sales is where you pay your dues," say many career counselors. They go on: "Few major companies will spend time recruiting undergraduates for mainstream brand, product, or general market management positions because very few BAs have the background and experience necessary to handle the broad ranging responsibilities entailed in such positions."[5]

* *Corporate recruiters confirm this view*. "We only hire MBAs for marketing positions, and usually only those who already have had some significant sales experience," says a salesperson at General Mills in Minneapolis. Adds a GE recruiter, "Students who want jobs in marketing but aren't willing to work in sales will be badly disappointed. Sales experience is a must."[6]

* *Sales today is data based, challenging, and among the most lucrative positions in any firm.* Certainly, a sales career is not for everyone, as the most effective sales pros have a strong work ethic, enjoy a competitive work environment, are extremely self-disciplined and enjoy working independently towards challenging goals. Integrity, humility and resiliency are also a must— get used to hearing "no."

❖ *Many use their sales experience to transition into brand, product, and general market management positions.*

❖ *Many others remain in sales.* Many who start in sales fall in love with the independence, flexible hours, competitive challenge to meet and surpass quotas, and significant compensation that naturally flow from success. They tend to remain in sales, typically rising to sales management within a few years, where compensation is even more lucrative. And, the door to product/brand management usually remains open.[7]

## Realize the false hope of sports marketing.

*Challenge:* Can you identify ten people who are neither All-Americans at some sport nor relatives of a team owner or athletic director who started in sports marketing and, after five years, are still in sports marketing? If you can do that, get advice from them and go for it.

*Example 1:* A former quality student (3.4 GPA) spent the last 10 years (yes, 10) bouncing from one sports marketing job to another. He picked up his MBA along the way from a quality institution (St. John's), and he currently works 60 hours per week as a sports team event planner for six teams at a Division I college. He earns $30,000 per year. That's not a misprint—and that's after 10 years and an MB. He is now 32 years old and ready to start over, finally giving up his sports marketing dream. This is more typical than not, except that most leave after one or two years—three years at most. Enough said. All is not lost—you can succeed in sports marketing, but, first, carefully consider the lesson below.

*Example 2:* An HR interviewer for a sports team, network, association or sporting goods manufacturer, while talking with a young potential candidate, asks, "Why should we hire you to work at XYZ Sports Company?" The candidate replies, "Because I love sports." The interviewer yells, "Next!" The interviewer thinks to herself, "What is so special about you? Most potential candidates love or at least like some dimension of sports. That's why the hours are long (60 per week) and the pay is low ($25,000 to $30,000 or less per year, even after several years). Go get some experience and bring something special to the table next time."

*Lesson:* If you are really committed to testing the waters in sports marketing, first get some significant marketing experience under your belt for five or more years, and then try the jump. Good luck!

# AN OVERVIEW OF
# MARKETING POSITIONS

Below, we have listed and briefly described many typical marketing positions. Some are entry-level positions, while others are more appropriate for marketing professionals with more experience. Since the entry-level positions lead to positions for the more experienced, consider both types of positions, with the assumption that with determination and diligent plans you should be able to gain the experience necessary for pursuing nearly any of these positions. The last section of this chapter provides real-life examples of how some specific young professionals have rather quickly migrated from entry-level marketing positions in only a few years. If you review these along with the examples provided earlier and below, you should be able to identify several potential career paths that might be right for you. Think of "right for you" as meaning both attractive to you and a position for which you feel qualified.[8] You can explore the sources in the Step 1 endnotes if you would like further perspectives on any particular position.[9]

## IN-COMPANY

### Typical in-company marketing positions

The exhibit below (next page) lists the more common marketing positions available in typical product or service companies.

The following list reviews some of the more typical in-company **longer-term marketing career positions** in marketing management, sales management and market research (in-company as opposed to working for an agency).[9]

*Marketing Managers.* Marketing managers work within individual consumer goods and service companies and within individual companies marketing business-to-business products, services, and solutions. This position oversees all aspects of a marketing plan and takes charge of creating and executing it from start to finish. Within specific companies, this role can also be a **brand manager** or **product manager,** where the employee is responsible for all marketing efforts of a particular brand or product line. Their primary responsibilities include:

- ❖ Identifying and monitoring customers and competitors;
- ❖ Searching out and identifying potential new offerings and target customers for existing offerings in order to continuously enhance market share and maintain overall sales growth;
- ❖ Designing, implementing, and monitoring product, distribution, sales, pricing, and promotion strategies as well as related support programs in ways that are ever-responsive to customer and competitor dynamics. Responses uniquely and continuously differentiate the company's various product and

service offerings from those of its competitors in order to foster the company's continuous growth of market share and sales.

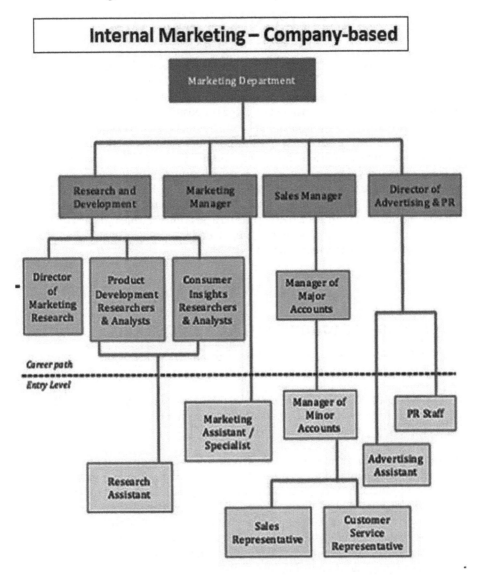

**For you?** Careers in product and brand management tend to attract well-motivated, high-potential, individuals who accept broad responsibilities with little supervision, communicate well, willingly travel, and thrive on constant change.[11] The job often comes with high pressure because brand managers must create marketing strategies that are better than those of the competitors.

## Others

❖ *Sales managers* direct the sales force, setting aggressive yet realistic sales and profit target goals and then designing and implementing appropriate stimulants and strategies for individual sales professionals and for the overall sales team in order to meet those goals.

❖

❖ *Market researchers and analysts within a company* run in-company research studies. Here the researchers identify (or are given) a market problem to explore. They then determine the appropriate research design (quantitative and qualitative), collect the data, analyze the data to generate results and related insights and recommendations, and, finally, communicate the results to appropriate parties.

  ❖ Monitoring and interpreting data is important for measuring the ongoing performance of the regular programs and strategies being implemented by the marketing management team.
  ❖ This also includes designing and making recommendations for modifying or refining current marketing programs and strategies.

❖ *Public relations: director of public relations.* The PR director and her/his staff are considered the spokespeople for the company. The goal of the PR department in any company is to portray the company in a flattering light, uphold its public image in a crisis, generate a positive buzz around the company and its business practices, and, of course, to publicize its products and services successfully. To do so, the public relations department manages communication with the media, consumers, employees, investors, and the general public.

  ❖ They write press releases to promote new products or to keep the investment community informed of business partnerships, financial results, or other company news.
  ❖ If based out of media relations, they will respond to information requests from journalist and pitch stories to the media.
  ❖ Anyone aiming to work in PR needs strong communication skills, with the ability to articulate well on paper and in person. They should be quick, creative thinkers with outgoing personalities who thrive by positively and persuasively responding to crises.[12]

## Typical in-company entry-level positions

Read and reflect on this overview of some of the more typical in-company entry-level marketing positions working for teams in marketing management, sales management and market research.

❖ Under marketing managers as a *marketing assistant*, a *marketing analyst*, or as an in-company *marketing specialist*, helping in one of the marketing program strategy areas such as product development, distribution, pricing, and/or advertising and promotion;

❖ Under sales managers as a company **sales representative** or in **customer service** (servicing existing customers by answering questions, troubleshooting problems, etc.);

❖ Under market research managers as a **marketing research analyst**, participating in data collection and analysis of either in-company research studies or monitoring the results of ongoing product, pricing, distribution, advertising/promotion programs, and strategies. This role is typically less glamorous and more technical, but it is a great way to gain experience in marketing research that will greatly benefit you in your career path.

# EXTERNAL AGENCIES

## Typical marketing agencies and positions

The exhibit below presents a summary of typical marketing positions available in external marketing roles at agencies.

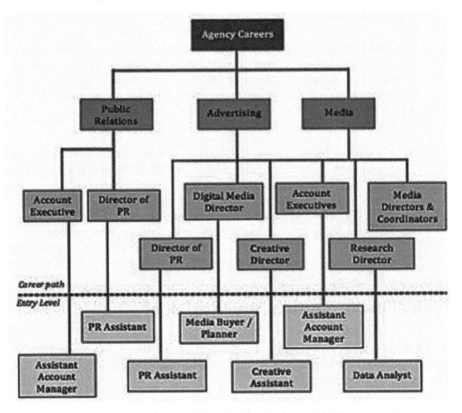

Here, we give you an overview of some of the more typical marketing career positions in advertising agencies, public relations agencies, and market research firms. By working for an agency rather than an individual company, your work will be externally driven (i.e., client-based, rather than in-house).

## Advertising agencies

**Advertising agencies** help their clients better communicate their market offerings to their target customers. This entails helping with research, product design, targeting tactics, creative process, budgeting funds, media plans, and media purchases, implementation, and measurement. Among the typical positions within an agency are: account management, creative, media, and research.

- ❖ *Account executives* manage client accounts but are only indirectly involved in the creative and media campaign output. They act as intermediary between the client account and the agency.
- ❖ *Research director* coordinates all research efforts with clients. They will often work with outside marketing research companies when conducting studies for clients.

- ❖ *Media directors and coordinators* decide how a campaign will reach customers through various types of media and serve as liaison between the client and the agencies' media buyers. This position often requires a lot of time allocating the fixed budget of a campaign among the most useful and successful media outlets.
- ❖ *Creative directors* work in a liaison role among clients, the account manager, and the agency's creative staff to ensure client-desired market positions and themes for its promotion efforts are translated effectively and efficiently into attention-grabbing advertisements.
- ❖ *Digital media directors* are rising in popularity and prevalence today given the rapid growth of digital marketing. They specialize in digital media outlets such as online advertising through Google, social media sites, webpage advertisements, and other digital platforms.
- ❖ *Promotions director* oversees a team that creates programs uniting advertising with purchase incentives such as special discounts, coupons, samples, gifts with purchase, rebates, and sweepstakes. It is not uncommon for an advertising agency to have a dedicated promotions team. To promote these programs, the team will often use digital, direct mail, telemarketing, in-store displays, assorted advertisements, product endorsements, and/or special kick-off events.[13] Marketing positions might include the leadership position of promotions director and, possibly for entry-level candidates, *promotions assistant.*

## Public relations agencies

**Public relations agencies** design, build, and maintain a positive public image for their individual clients, supporting such efforts with regular press releases and programs to promote that image. They strive to portray the client in a flattering light, uphold its public image in a crisis, generate a positive buzz around its company and business practices, and publicize its products and services.

* **PR account executives** interface and manage all aspects of public relations with specific assigned clients. Again, this role functions as the intermediary between the client and the agency.
* **The *director of public relations*** manages overall agency PR business, including managing accounts, generating new business, and ensuring successful performance throughout the agency's PR practice, from account relations with individual clients to the performance of PR assistants in executing PR directives from managers and account executives.

## Digital marketing agencies

* *Learning by doing has been the norm in digital marketing.* Because digital marketing is relatively new, few marketing grads—or college grads in general—have had any courses specifically in digital marketing (estimated as fewer than 10 percent in one study).[14] Most successful digital marketing professionals become experts on the job (i.e., learned by doing).
* *Digital agencies often require an internship before the entry-level position.* In light of this lack of digital marketing course experience, and in the view of most agencies, most new college grads simply do not have the requisite digital experience and skills to qualify for mainstream digital positions with agencies of any sort. To address this, many agencies now offer valuable training internships that can and often do lead to full-time job offers. See sources referenced in the endnotes for tips on capturing entry-level opportunities in digital marketing.[15]
* *Digital is transforming marketing today.* Marketing and related career opportunities are evolving as the volume and depth of data on consumers (often referred to as "Big Data") explode each year. The leading marketing companies today—e.g., manufacturers, retailers, advertising and marketing agencies, and consultants—are developing and using sophisticated analytics to tease out the meaning of that data. This is revolutionizing both the nature and importance of marketing today, bringing marketing professionals into central focus for forward-looking firms that want to grow and succeed.
* Consider a few examples of the exciting and dynamic challenges a digital marketer might face today:[16]

  * Position a company's brand in the marketplace, competing for customers across mobile, web, social media, and print channels;
  * Research target customer interactions with the company's website to uncover the trends: where they are, what they do, what they value most, and how to convert and maintain their loyalty;
  * Turn research data on customer awareness, engagement and other interactions with specific social media platforms into actionable marketing insights, goals, and strategies;
  * Create and strategize multi-channel marketing campaigns, from print pieces to Pinterest, Instagram, Snapchat, and others;
  * Experiment with emerging technology and new social media platforms to cultivate loyal customers and brand enthusiasts;

* Planning and buying paid search advertising campaigns across Facebook, Twitter, and LinkedIn

* Entry-level marketing opportunities in digital, including with digital agencies. Young graduates who have been growing up in an ever-more digital world have a significant advantage over veterans who are presently in the most important marketing roles. Agencies and companies are recognizing this and creating important, new, high-visibility entry-level digital marketing opportunities that bring with them more responsibility (and commensurate compensation) than traditional entry-level marketing positions. *Note, however, that they often require internships.*

## Market research companies

Marketing research companies are experts in the area of research for companies. They provide insight and research on companies' products and marketing strategies. Below is a diagram of different areas of marketing research companies.

Marketing research companies provide many alternative services, such as:

* Gathering syndicated data (e.g., in-store data auto-collection, focus groups, wired households, etc.);
* Interpreting and disseminating syndicated data to individual clients, exploring for customer insights to help develop;
* Refining and testing various marketing program dimensions (e.g., advance testing of prospective new product types/sizes/colors, alternative pricing strategies, alternative promotional themes, use of alternative media, variations media frequency and timing);
* Crunching massive data sets (data mines) to tease out the most meaningful and useful data and trends;
* Conducting full-scale ad hoc custom studies for individual clients on any marketing program dimension; and
* Acting as sub-contractors for in-company market research departments to help with research design, data collection, data analysis, and interpretation for specific research studies.
* Typical leadership positions in market research agencies are:

  * **Market research director**, who oversees the overall business, keeping it on track;
  * **Account managers**, who maintain and build business with individual companies that use the agency's research services; and,
  * **Research supervisors**, who run individual research efforts from start to finish, allocating financial and manpower resources and keeping research efforts on track and within budget.

The typical entry-level position in market research agencies is as a *research analyst*, who runs individual dimensions of the research, including data collection, analysis, and interpretation. They may also aid in communicating final results to the client.

## Marketing consulting companies

Marketing consulting companies cover any of the potential services identified above for advertising, public relations, market research, or digital agencies.

# Typical marketing agency entry-level positions

- ❖ *Media planner and buyer:* Identifies and purchases specific ad media, frequency, timing, etc. to help the clients reach their marketing objectives most efficiently within a fixed budget.
- ❖ *Data analyst:* Completes basic number crunching to identify tendencies and trends, and then reports those results to internal agency personnel (and eventually directly to clients as well). Uses sophisticated statistical techniques to uncover consumer insights for designing or refining various dimensions of clients' marketing programs, then reporting those results.
- ❖ *Market research assistant*: Assists with any step in specific contracted research studies.
    - ❖ **For example, this might involve helping senior market researchers determine the appropriate design (quantitative and qualitative), collect the data, analyze the data to generate results and related insights and recommendations, and, finally, participate in communicating the results to appropriate parties.**
    - ❖ **The ideal candidate for a market research position is a person who possesses both qualitative and quantitative analytical**

ability, since the job depends on your ability to gather data from human subjects, crunch numbers, and interpret the results accurately.

- ❖ *Public relations assistant*: Help PR directors and account managers identify, translate, communicate, and monitor a client's desired image with the public through research, targeted custom press releases, press coordination, and events.[17]
- ❖ *Creative assistant*: Translate the client's desired marketing themes into attention-grabbing ad designs for print, captive media (radio/TV), outdoor, digital, or other media. Position favors those with imagination to burn and with an extensive portfolio from formal design classes and experiences. This person works for the creative director, typically on unique creative assignments for specific clients.

# RETAIL MANAGEMENT

## Typical retail management positions

The exhibit below displays an array of retail stores as well as a summary of positions in retail management.

*Retail Managers*. Retail managers oversee all store functions. They are responsible for creating a layout within the store that will assist in increasing sales and productivity. Basic tasks they perform to do so are moving items around the store and creating attractive displays. Along with these responsibilities, retail managers are also in charge handling their employees. This entails hiring and training employees as well as terminating those who are not performing up to standards.[18] Other responsibilities include:

- ❖ Handling the vendors and the buying process;
- ❖ Managing inventory;
- ❖ Interacting with customers and responding to any questions, complaints or comments they have regarding the store;
- ❖ Creating and implementing sales and promotion programs
- ❖ Overseeing budgets, expenses, sales figures, and profits.[19]

*For you?* Retail management is a profession that demands juggling many responsibilities at a time. Professionals in this area must start at the bottom and work their way up the ladder. They are highly motivated individuals that are good at communicating, have strong negotiation and customer service skills, and are patient and friendly. Hours for a retail manager are usually outside of a typical 9-5 timeframe. Stores are meant to serve the general public who are working during this time; therefore, evenings and weekends are the busier times for stores and managers must work during these non-traditional hours to maximize their impact and effectiveness. In order to reach a position as retail manager, workers must first learn all of the ins and outs of retail and be willing to relocate upon promotion.

## Others

❖ *Corporate Marketing Managers* are responsible for developing the brand of the actual retail company.  They must work on developing creative integrated marketing campaigns targeted at the customers.  Their focus is to increase market share within the company's retail division through advertising and media plans.[22]

❖ *Senior Buyers and Planners* are two positions that often go hand in hand. Buyers are responsible for building the product selection within the store as well as driving sales through product development, assortment selection, pricing, presentation and promotion. They work with planners who typically oversee a specific product category. The planners must be aware of customers' wants and are responsible for getting those desired products into the stores.[23]

❖ *In-store sales force managers* direct the sales force, setting aggressive yet realistic sales and profit target goals and then designing and implementing appropriate stimulants and strategies for individual sales professionals and for the overall sales team in order to meet those goals.

❖ *Operations* **managers** are in charge of more than one store location. They are typically in charge of a number of stores within a region. Tasks that operations managers must perform are ensuring their stores are staffed correctly, controlling costs of inventory, and instructing store managers on how to organize the store and what kinds of merchandising layouts to use.24 Many of the responsibilities are similar to retail managers, but over more than one store.

## Typical entry-level positions in retail management

Here is a review some of the typical entry-level positions in retail management.

❖ Under corporate marketing managers as a *marketing assistant,* aiding in creating marketing campaigns and developing the branding for the retail company;

❖ Under retail managers as a *salesman* or a *retail store assistant manager,* helping to run operations within the store and gain a full understanding of all aspects of the retail industry;

❖ Under buyers and planners as an *assistant buyer* or a *planning analyst,* working under senior buyers/planners or a merchandise specialist to assist in product development and new product implementation;

❖ Under sales force managers as a company *sales representative* or in *customer service* (servicing existing customers by answering questions, troubleshooting problems, etc.);

❖ Under operations managers as a *retail store associate* or *retail store manager*, working to keep track of the store's inventory and ensuring the store's layout and displays are set up properly and efficiently.

# EXAMPLES OF ENTRY-LEVEL MARKETING POSITIONS

Appearing below are specific, actual positions now held by marketing students who graduated anywhere from one to three years ago. A review of these examples might spark an initial interest. Of course, dozens of other possibilities exist as well, but these initial examples might help you start your exploration for an entry-level marketing position that is right for you.

- Company brand manager/Beam-Suntory assistant brand manager
- Product innovation specialist/Nielsen demand and innovation analyst
- Advertising (agency) media planner/Starcom media lanner
- Digital marketing analyst/Accenture interactive digital analyst
- Digital marketing sales representative/Google account manager
- Market research associate/Eli Lilly market research associate
- Retail analyst/Target retail business analyst
- Retail account manager for consumer products company/General Mills customer account manager
- Business technology sales executive/AT&T client solutions executive
- Sales representative in the beverage industry/Miller-Coors craft beer rep
- Technology solutions consultant/Salesforce(.com) solutions engineer
- Customer service representative/FinancialForce.com (FCC) implementation consultant
- Graphic designer/Red Caffeine marketing and technology

## Company brand manager

Sarah Johnson began her career at Beam Suntory in Chicago, one of the world's leading premium spirits suppliers, in 2013 as a summer marketing intern. Following graduation, she returned full-time as an assistant brand manager on the SkinnyGirl cocktails business. In this position, her efforts focused on generating, analyzing, and interpreting data to help the SkinnyGirl marketing team to develop plans and strategies to continuously expand brand sales.

Sarah then transitioned to a role as manager in commercial marketing across Beam Suntory's vodka portfolio. Her job focuses on shopper and experiential marketing efforts for both Pinnacle Vodka and EFFEN Vodka. She drives the strategic development of channel-specific programs that are rooted in insights and directly linked to commercial plans for each brand. On any given day, she works with her cross-functional partners in brand management, insights, and field marketing to develop national programs that drive consumer engagement at the point of sale. Sarah enjoys working in marketing with a commercial lens to understand a different perspective of the business, while also working with creative agencies to help develop unique campaigns for retail distributors.

## Product innovation

Kelly Branson was a professional service, custom practice intern at Nielsen during summer 2013. There, she analyzed data to inform clients about optimal promotional strategies. After graduation in 2014, she returned to Nielsen and has since been working in Nielsen's innovation practice.

As a demand analyst, Kelly works with a vast array of data generated through Nielsen proprietary platforms. She interprets that data to draw consumer insights, manages internal timelines, and develops and writes actionable and insightful recommendations counseling clients on how to develop, prioritize, optimize, and execute new product launches. The goal is to help clients beat the odds and launch long-term, relevant, and profitable new products. She has worked on projects for clients like MillerCoors, Kraft, and Tyson. These projects include optimizing positioning to maximize interest in a new ale, constructing a snacking category landscape, and determining share-maximizing price strategy.

## Advertising (Agency) media planner

After working in media planning at Starcom MediaVest Group for about 15 months, Jody Stacy transitioned into her role as media investment supervisor. There she works with Tapestry, the multicultural arm of Starcom, where she specializes in total market media buying across TV and digital. Her first account was fabric care for Procter & Gamble; after that, she moved to Starcom's Kellogg's account, for which she helps manage frozen and snack brands.

During a typical day on the Kellogg's team, Jody ensures that her team is on track with their campaign launch timeline, along with buying digital displays, video, and social media for her brands. Whether it's making sure brand budgets are accurate, emailing potential partners to finalize plans, or speaking with clients to answer any questions they have, her primary role is to guarantee that the overall digital buying process flows smoothly. She also helps manage live campaigns to make sure they meet all of Kellogg's performance benchmarks. For TV, Jody manages Kellogg's Hispanic budgets and the Hispanic TV Upfront for Kellogg's. Similar to digital, this job also consists of keeping track of budgets, as well as working with different Kellogg's teams to ensure TV plans are received and properly loaded in Starcom systems for the new broadcast year.

## Digital marketing analyst

After graduating, Katherine Walker accepted a job with Accenture Interactive (AI) in Chicago to work on Google AdWords projects, and other roles involving SEO (search engine optimization), social media, eCommerce, and site heuristics with various Accenture clients.

More specifically, Katherine manages an AdWords account daily for a Canadian retail client in addition to running their paid Facebook advertising campaigns. She has contributed to an SEO project for a cellular company and a social listening project for another cellular customer, and she also works on internal design projects for other sectors of Accenture. Katherine interacts with clients in all of her projects, even as an analyst, and loves the diversity and wide range of responsibilities that her position provides each day.

## Digital marketing sales representative

Monica Lopez started at Google in Ann Arbor, Michigan, where she worked with small- to medium-sized businesses to grow their online presence through Google's digital marketing platforms. She now works in Chicago as an account manager with four major business and industrial markets, including Chevron, Northern Tool & Equipment, Boeing, and John Deere.

Monica's current role centers on developing online advertising strategies for her clients utilizing the Google suite of online advertising solutions. As an account manager, her days involve managing relationships between clients and ad agencies, advising and consulting on advertising strategies, overseeing the tactical operations of ad campaigns, and overseeing internal reporting to upper management and key stakeholders for all of her accounts.

## Market research associate

Danielle Druger began her career with Eli Lilly & Company in Indianapolis. She started in Lilly's rotational program, the Lilly Marketing Academy, in which she completed two six-month rotations—one on an insulin product in the Diabetes Business Unit and one on Cialis in the BioMedicines Business Unit. In July 2015, she began her full-time role as a market research associate for the Alzheimer's Platform. In this role, she focuses her efforts on Lilly's Phase III drug called Solanezumab (targeted for early-stage Alzheimer's patients) and a diagnostic imaging tool called Amyvid that tests for the presence of Alzheimer's. As a market researcher, Danielle works with the brand team to understand the business decision (i.e., what the team will change based on research findings), develops a study using both qualitative and quantitative techniques, and analyzes findings to provide nonbiased, tested results for Eli Lilly brand and product managers. She is proud to be involved in shaping the thinking for a drug that could positively impact the lives of millions of people living with Alzheimer's across the globe—more than 6 million in the USA alone.

## Retail analyst

Dana Wilson interned with Target as a merchandise planning business analyst following her junior year, gaining valuable experience managing and owning inventory in the apparel division.

Reflecting a very positive internship experience, Dana accepted an offer from Target and returned to the apparel division shortly after graduation as a business analyst. Shortly thereafter, she began monitoring and analyzing a vast array of apparel sales and sales trend data. Based on her findings and assessment of constantly changing trends, Dana orders and allocates millions of dollars of apparel inventory nationwide for each new season. She stays in constant communication with vendors and other cross-functional teams to ensure seamless execution of inventory allocation.

## Retail account manager for consumer products company

Joe Sullivan joined General Mills as a business management associate and is now a GMI customer account manager, focusing on the Jewel-Osco account.

In his Chicago-based account manager role, Joe manages a $6-million budget and has full responsibility for 350+ General Mills (GMI) products at Jewel-Osco, a retail chain with 184 stores throughout Illinois and Indiana. What excites Joe most is analyzing and interpreting raw data on sales to gather insights on consumer sales, which he then applies in his negotiations with and presentations for his distribution customers. His role requires a deep understanding of the financials (profit margin, dollar volume, unit elasticity, annual brand growth data) in order to package and present such data to his customers in a way that stimulates immediate action. Joe sees himself at General Mills for the long term, given his natural affinity for the food industry, his regular exposure to high-level GMI executives, and projected opportunities for regular promotions.

## Business-to-business technology sales executive

Jackson McGovern began his career at AT&T in their Business Sales Leadership Development Program (BSLDP). After the one-year BSLDP program in Atlanta, he moved to Chicago as a client solutions executive. In that role, he has been responsible for selling AT&T's entire product portfolio of wired and mobile applications to small- and medium-sized businesses in the Chicago market. He is also responsible for business sales at eight AT&T retail stores in downtown Chicago in addition to mentoring new AT&T BSLDP participants.

Emily Stanson transitioned through the same programs as Jackson, becoming a client solutions executive (formerly called "account manager") in the New York City market. After two years, she became senior product development manager–mobility, helping develop mobility products for emerging business markets in Dallas. Currently, she is the lead product marketing development manager for security solutions for AT&T.

## Sales representative in the beverage industry

Courtney Nelms works as an on premise sales representative for MillerCoors. In her job, she brings the MillerCoors beverage portfolio alive across various bars in Chicago. Her primary challenge is expanding the distribution of Miller-Coors' ever-increasing portfolio of craft beers into craft-focused pubs in the Chicago craft pub market. On a day-to-day basis, she sells new products to the bars, arranges beer dinners and consumer experiences, and works with bar owners to quantify their business while consulting with them on the profitability of various MillerCoors beers. Courtney enjoys keeping up with the ever-changing landscape of the beer industry and is intrigued by the interlinking challenges of beer marketers, beer sales teams, and bar owners.

## Solutions consultant at a technology company

Tom Baker began working for Dunnhumby in 2014. There, he helped retailers and manufacturers understand their shoppers and drive a customer-first strategy. After a year, he transitioned to a solutions engineer position at Salesforce Marketing Cloud in Chicago. At Salesforce.com, Tom helps multiple clients use the Salesforce Marketing Cloud platform and tools to access and interpret huge amounts of data in order to enhance their marketing programs, customer relations, and related sales.

Tom's day-to-day challenge involves building close personal relationships with his customers by helping them generate more data on their customers and make better use of that data to enhance their marketing programs. Over the past six months as a solutions engineer, Tom contributed to activities such as: leading a strategic workshop with NFL executives to help them design better strategies for getting more fans to games; demonstrating a Salesforce tool for a nonprofit company to help them find more volunteers; and consulting with an online real estate company to connect them with more buyers and sellers using social media. Every day is different, and there's always a new and exciting challenge. Tom particularly enjoys working in the sweet spot at the intersection of marketing, technology, sales, and consulting.

## Customer service representative

Kelly Lewis works as a customer service representative in the role of implementation consultant for FinancialForce.com (FFC). FFC provides cloud enterprise resource planning solutions in accounting, billing, human capital management, supply chain management, customer relationship management, and other areas.

After six months of training in a variety of FFC solutions, Kelly now works the phones helping FFC clients implement solutions in the SCM and CRM spaces. She has an outgoing personality and loves talking with FFC clients and helping them with questions about implementing their contracted solutions.

Kelly has continued her training so she can eventually help clients implement other FFC solutions. She loves the opportunity to learn about so many dimensions of business (e.g., the list of FFC offerings above). She is also very excited to be building a network of contacts with the FFC customers she is helping. Kelly anticipates she will eventually migrate into one specific functional area at FFC, either continuing her trouble-shooting role, moving into implementation per se, or becoming an FCC sales professional. That said, she (like may FCC consultants in the past) might also receive a new offer from one of the customers she is helping.

## Graphic designer

Lauren Holiday began her career as a graphic designer through a series of unpaid internships, two of which she completed during her senior year of college. These supplemented her classes and acted as a learning experience that went beyond the classroom. Upon graduation, Lauren took another internship for Keystroke Graphics/Wedding Guide Chicago. This husband-wife joint company helped her gain more experience in the design world and build up her portfolio.

Lauren landed her first paid position as a junior graphic designer for DKI Services and was promoted to graphic designer within the first year. DKI is a disaster restoration contracting organization, and Lauren completed a diverse range of projects for both internal and external customers of the company. Some common projects she worked on included business cards, folders, brochures, letterheads, logos, presentations, booths, pop-up displays, and banners. She also worked on branding development throughout the three branches of the company to have consistency in all areas of their design work.

Three years later, Lauren transitioned to Red Caffeine Marketing and Technology as a graphic designer, where she serves as the lead designer on seven client accounts. In her work, Lauren always tries to think about who her audience is and consider whether her designs make sense to the average person. On a typical day, she juggles multiple projects, from creating a tradeshow design for one client to building an entirely new website for another.

# IN CLOSING

One of the best aspects of a marketing career is that there are so many routes you can take! That said, deciding a favored industry or position is a challenging task.

In Step 1 we have reviewed a great deal of information on various career paths in marketing. The purpose of this discussion is to stimulate thinking about which careers sound most exciting and realistic for you.

We suggest you take some time to review the material here and elsewhere and think about what kind of career you'd like to have and which aspects of a job are most important to you.[26] Once you have an idea of where you'd like to go, move on to the next steps to prepare your materials and then identify and pursue attractive potential opportunities. The next steps in this book should help you in your search for that dream entry-level marketing position.

## Step #1 REVIEW QUESTIONS

❖

1. What two questions should you ask yourself to help focus your job search?
2. Out of the dozen specific examples of entry-level position reviewed, which did you find most interesting?
3. What percentage of digital marketers have a business/marketing degree? Why so low? What is the implication of that? If digital marketing is of potential interest, what can one do to qualify oneself for consideration?
4. What is the difference between advertising and marketing?
5. Why are advertising jobs difficult to land and why do they start out paying so low?
6. If someone wants to become a brand, product or general marketing manager, how would you suggest they pursue that goal?
7. What are the advantages of starting one's marketing career in sales?
8. Identify 10 people who started in sports marketing and after five years are still in sports marketing.
9. Take a look at the marketing career position organization charts. In any one of the organization charts, plot an attractive, realistic potential career path for yourself.
10. With your own career in mind, what would you regard as the advantages and disadvantages of starting your career in an individual company, in some dimension of retailing, or in one of the different types of agencies described.

1 Abstracted from allbusinessschools.com/business-careers/marketing/job-description/

2 This brief section synthesizes, paraphrases, and, in some instances, expands upon insights from Laura Lake, a marketing expert in About Money marketing.about.com/od/careersinmarketing/a/marketinginternships.htm

3 marketing.about.com/cs/marketingjobs/a/breakinmrktg.htm and aiesec.ca/blog/what-education-backgrounds-do-marketers-have/

4 marketing.about.com/cs/advertising/a/marketvsad.htm—Marketing vs. Advertising: What's the Difference? Updated January 31, 2015.

5 careercast.com/career-news/myth-marketing-careers

6 careercast.com/career-news/myth-marketing-careers

7 Warning: After 3-5 years, if you are good at sales, you may well be wearing an attractive set of "golden handcuffs"—making $130K, 140K, 150K or more per year, versus the 100K that entry-level product and brand managers are making. Who wants a pay cut? Who wants an 8-5 or 8-8 day, when your time has been your own for the past 3-5 years?

8 allbusinessschools.com/business-careers/marketing/job-description/; marketing.about.com/cs/marketingjobs/a/careers.htm

9 For more information, see (2016) Eric Siebert, Careers in Marketing, The Comprehensive Guide to Traditional and Digital Marketing Careers – available on Amazon.

9 allbusinessschools.com/business-careers/marketing/job-description/

11 marketing.about.com/cs/marketingjobs/a/careers.htm

12 marketing.about.com/cs/marketingjobs/a/careers.htm

13 marketing.about.com/cs/marketingjobs/a/careers.htm

14 aiesec.ca/blog/what-education-backgrounds-do-marketers-have/

15 For tips on how to find success in digital marketing, see toprankblog.com/2013/07/digital-marketing-jobs/; and this 11-minute video youtube.com/watch?v=inMaGwo-shE

16 allbusinessschools.com/business-careers/marketing/

17 marketing.about.com/cs/marketingjobs/a/careers.htm

18 http://www.monster.com/jobs/q-retail-manager-jobs.aspx

19 http://www.careerealism.com/retail-management-career/

22 https://corporate.target.com/careers/career-areas/advertising-and-marketing

23 https://corporate.target.com/careers/career-areas/Brand-Management-Buying-Planning

24 http://work.chron.com/basic-job-skills-retail-operations-manager-25610.html

26 For example, see (2016) Eric Siebert, Careers in Marketing, The Comprehensive Guide to Traditional and Digital Marketing Careers—available on Amazon.

# STEP 2
# PREPARING MATERIALS
# FOR YOUR SEARCH

## QUICK START

The previous section provided some perspectives and details on the wide variety of available entry-level marketing positions. Once you have a pretty good idea of the type of entry-level position you might like to pursue, before diving into the search process, it makes sense to prepare materials that you will use to 'sell yourself' to prospective employers. These materials include your:

* ❖ Resume;
* ❖ Leadership (or "proof") stories; and
* ❖ Any supporting documentation that may be relevant for your targeted position (e.g., a portfolio if you are hoping for an entry-level position in any area of design or other creative position).

This section chapter reviews each of these items. You will also want to prepare yourself for the interview process itself, which we cover in Step 5, "Interview Strategies and Tips."

## RESUME

Remember that your resume is only one of hundreds competing to be noticed for consideration for the position. In order to stand out, make sure that your resume is formatted in a unique way with great content. It is also important to structure your resume in a way that will be quick and easy to review.

## LEADERSHIP STORIES

Leadership stories are a crucial tool to prepare for your job search. They are stories that exemplify your accomplishments and can serve as a degree of proof that you do indeed possess certain important qualities that employers are looking for. They are great as a complement to your resume as they help the recruiter or hiring manager get a much truer picture of who you really are. These stories will also help you in all phases of your interviews for your 'dream' entry-level position.

## SUPPORTING DOCUMENTATION

You might need additional documents when applying for certain types of entry-level marketing positions. For example, many design-based and creative positions will require examples of your work in order to get a better idea of the type of work you can create. If you are looking into positions like these, it is helpful to develop and regularly enhance a portfolio of all the pieces that you have created. The portfolio could be designs you have made or pieces of writing you have crafted. Here are some examples of portfolios that you might emulate:

- ❖ chasesarahchase.com
- ❖ cargocollective.com/ericwebster
- ❖ melaniedaveid.com
- ❖ lesleycstevenson.wordpress.com

# YOUR RESUME:
# SOME PRINCIPLES AND TIPS[1]

Hundreds of people may be competing for the same position as you. In most instances, recruiters simply do not have time to review the details of each resume submitted. To make their task more manageable, recruiters set screening criteria to cull the large group of resumes and applications down to a more manageable subset. Depending upon how many have applied for a specific position, even this "small stack" may include 50 to 100 or more resumes. How do you make this 'short stack?'

- ❖ Perhaps the most effective way to make the short stack is to get a sponsor—someone within the company who recommends you. We cover this topic in depth in later steps.
- ❖ A more obvious way to make the short stack is by having some outstanding content front and center on your resume—standout material that is immediately and clearly visible to the reviewer.

Making the short stack is the just first challenge. Your resume has about 20 seconds, maximum, to impress the recruiter. Why? It's simple—a recruiter can't possibly look in detail through each of as many as 50 to 100 or more resumes. You increase your chances of getting a careful look by making the recruiter's job easier. This first section of the chapter provides some tips for doing just that—stimulating the recruiter to pull your resume and see the best of your background and accomplishments in that very fast 20-second scan of your resume.

# RESUME DESIGN

## Make your resume stand out.

Recruiters and others involved in the hiring process see hundreds of resumes competing for the same position—typically hundreds of look-a-like, boring resumes. Step it up! Be creative and unique. *Dare to stand out.* Drawing attention to your resume will increase your chances of getting noticed right off the bat. Later in this Step 2 we provide some examples of some uniquely appealing resumes

## Structure your resume to make it easy to review.

### Use bullet points.

It is impossible for recruiters to scan a resume quickly if it is full of paragraphs. Bullets help recruiters quickly scan for the key information they need.

### List most important and recent accomplishments first.

Recruiters only scan the first few bullets for each school or work experience. If your most important accomplishment is in the sixth bullet point, the recruiter is unlikely to see it. Put your most recent and most impressive internships, awards, and accomplishments first to maximize the chances that the recruiter will review them in the few seconds she or he has to spend on your resume.

## Examples

Consider the resumes below. Note the creativity incorporated in the look of some of them. Which types of resumes do you think will draw immediate attention? It's pretty obvious which ones stand out.

What does your resume look like? Apart from content, how does it draw attention and express your individuality? Hundreds of designs with different formatting are instantly available on the Web.[2]

*Each of the resumes below has particular strengths and weaknesses. A couple of notes about each of them:*

❖ **Resume 1:** This resume is loaded with great content. Her work history indicates the applicant is qualified for the position; however, the standard design doesn't help the content stand out. Furthermore, the category "experience" is vague. Label your resume sections with greater specificity.

❖ **Resume 2:** This applicant successfully incorporates nuance and detail to each of the sections. Separating professional experience from leadership experience is a smart idea—it helps to make the resume easier to navigate. The addition of "relevant coursework" at the top of the page connects educational experiences to work potential. This thoughtful touch conveys skills a job applicant has that work experience might not suggest. That section also establishes a great talking point for the interview process.

❖ **Resume 3:** Like the first two examples, resume 3 has very plain formatting, and it will most likely be lost in the stack of job applications. Still, this resume is still loaded with an abundance of great work experience. A unique addition to this resume is the "honors" section at the top. This offers an easy way to show off some of your accomplishments that you definitely want the interviewer to know about.

❖ **Resume 4:** This resume perfectly exemplifies how to add a little extra visual appeal to your resume. The format is simple, but it still makes the resume stand out. That said, be careful not to make the mistake of sacrificing content for creative design. As you can see, the experience section of resume 4 is quite barren compared to that of the three earlier examples. Having a unique design will draw attention to your resume, but the content will get you the interview!

❖ **Resume 5:** The job applicant who created this resume is definitely someone who thinks outside the box. There are a several unique aspects to the resume that are eye-catching, such as the "Skills" visual and the "About Me" section. Unfortunately, this is another example where content is sacrificed in attempt to make the resume stand out—balance between content and creativity would improve the applicant's chance of continuing through the recruitment process.

❖ **Resume 6:** Resume 6 also illustrates a very easy formatting technique that sets the resume apart. In this example, the "Skills" section is entertaining because the information provided is somewhat unusual for a resume.  Be cautious not to overdo the attention-grabbing techniques. Seek a 'golden-mean' between look and content.

❖ **Resume 7:** The last example does a great job of combining creativity with great content. The images enhance the resume perfectly while still allowing enough space to feature the applicant's abundant of relevant experience. The unique "numbers" section also allows the reviewer to get to know the applicant a little bit better with some fun facts on her life.

## Resume 1

### Sandra Rust

123 Drury Lane ◆ Bakerstown, IN 46637 ◆ (555) 222-1000 ◆ srust@gmail.com

#### EDUCATION & HONORS

**University of Notre Dame**  Notre Dame, IN
*Bachelor of Business Administration – Major: Marketing    Minor: Chinese, Italian*  May 2016
Dean's List-Fall 2012, Fall 2013, Spring 2014, Fall 2014  GPA: 3.85/4.00

#### EXPERIENCE

**Harmonia** – Notre Dame, IN  August 2013-Present
*Music Director*
  ◆ Led practices and musical performances, composed musical pieces, and made executive decisions
*Public Relations Manager*
  ◆ Established Instagram page and maintained other social channels to increase group awareness and broadcast events

**Nielsen** – Chicago, IL  June 2015-August 2015
*Professional Services Intern – Sales Effectiveness Assortment Team*
  ◆ Examined why Base Sales Dollars is a more fitting input than Total Sales for the Assortment team's model
  ◆ Conducted an internal validation study on our team's model and determined it has a 86% weighted accuracy
  ◆ Revamped 47 DFBeta clusters list and created 20 new clusters, which will allow for more accurate client solutions
  ◆ Devised an on-campus Nielsen ambassador program and presented it to the SVP of HR, SVP of Diversity, and VP of HR

**Undergraduate Women in Business** – Notre Dame, IN  August 2013-May 2015
*Secretary*
  ◆ Planned and executed events aimed at providing business insights and networking opportunities for women
  ◆ Built a new UWIB website to improve participation and understanding of the club and to promote events

**Brew Werks** – South Bend, IN  August 2014-December 2014
*Consultant*
  ◆ Created and implemented a business plan to guide future growth for a new brewpub in South Bend
  ◆ Conducted marketing research to determine what events and promotions will increase customer traffic

**Student International Business Council** – Notre Dame, IN  January 2013-December 2014
*Project Leader, Nielsen Marketing Group*
  ◆ Investigated ways for Mars Chocolate/Candy to gain a better understanding of its current portfolio in the snacking
    world and plan for future innovation by increasing its presence in the outdoor enthusiast and elderly markets
*Member, Tassimo Marketing Group*
  ◆ Formulated on-campus implementation of Tassimo, Kraft's coffee brewer, into the mid-sized college campus market
  ◆ Scrutinized the strengths and weakness of the marketing strategy and presented findings to Nielsen

**Cardinal Health** – Dublin, OH  June 2014-August 2014
*Hospital Sales & Services Marketing Intern*
  ◆ Recommended ideal digital channels for B2B and devised campaigns targeting hospital supply chain decision makers
  ◆ Examined correlation between 2 hospital segmentation sets and presented hospital targeting plan to VP of Marketing
  ◆ Identified educational opportunities at AHRMM regional chapters and coordinated 3 speakers for upcoming events

**Morris Inn** – Notre Dame, IN  January 2014-February 2014
*Marketing Consultant*
  ◆ Assessed how to increase restaurant traffic within the local community, Notre Dame faculty, and students
  ◆ Presented proposal and social media strategy to the General Manager and Chief of Marketing for the Morris Inn

#### SERVICE

**Appalachia Service Seminar** – Hurley, VA  October 2013
*Participant*
  ◆ Provided renewed hope by refurbishing an impoverished, older woman's house and constructing a volunteer building

**Columbus Academy Service Board** – Gahanna, OH  May 2011-June 2012
*Vice-President*
  ◆ Organized food, clothing and blood drives, which served 32 families and generated 30 units of blood
  ◆ Facilitated weekly meetings, advocated participation in service activities, and supervised service events

#### SKILLS

*Language:* Intermediate Mandarin Chinese • Intermediate Italian
*Technical:* Proficient in Microsoft Word, PowerPoint, Excel, Access, SPSS

## Resume 2

### Joseph Johnson
Current: 123 Drury Lane      Bakerstown, IN 46637

Permanent: 20 Ginger Bread Trail • Joytown, PA 15821 • 555.222.1000 • jjohnson234@nd.edu

**Education:**

| | |
|---|---|
| **University of Notre Dame**—Notre Dame, IN | May 2016 |
| **University of Notre Dame London Program** – London, England | Fall 2014 |

Bachelors of Business Administration
**Major:** Marketing  **Minor:** Constitutional Studies
**Major GPA:** 3.8/4.0 **Cumulative GPA:** 3.46/4.0
**Honors:** Dean's List (Fall 2014), Frank J. Soler Leadership Award (Spring 2015), Fisher Hall Brotherhood Award (Spring 2015)
**Relevant Coursework:** Building Great Brands, Marketing Planning for Growth, Marketing Research, Marketing Analytics

**Professional Experience:**

Chick-fil-A, Inc. – Atlanta, GA                                                                           **May - August 2015**
**Marketing Intern**
- Advanced partnership between Chick-fil-A, Inc. and the College Football Hall of Fame through collaborative events such as the inaugural Ultimate Father/Son Campout, which hosted over 250 Grand Prize Winners from nearly 100 Atlanta Chick-fil-A Restaurants overnight at the Hall for an unforgettable fan experience
- Designed and executed the engagement plan for Chick-fil-A's "Frosted Lemonade Spectacular", a first-of-its-kind promotion which built brand awareness in the Midwest Region

University of Notre Dame—Notre Dame, IN                                                                     **Spring 2015**
**Marketing Research Assistant**
- Researched consumer responses related to pricing transparency and the effect of one's gender on subconscious preferences towards even and odd-numbered prices
- Worked part-time throughout the spring semester to assist in editing and conducting surveys and analyzing data

Saratoga Performing Arts Center (SPAC) — Saratoga Springs, NY                                              **May - August 2014**
**Marketing Assistant**
- Drafted and updated trade agreements submitted to Corporate Sponsors exchanging products and services valued over $30,000
- Managed and executed the distribution of 25,000 season program brochures to hundreds of local businesses and organizations throughout the Northeast
- Analyzed data from surveys taken by board members and customers to aid in the strategic planning of SPAC's 50th Anniversary, taking place Summer 2015

University of Notre Dame—Notre Dame, IN                                                          **Fall 2012 - Spring 2014**
**Student International Business Council (SIBC)**
- Provided to Target executives an evaluation of the marketing campaign used for their new Mobile Application, Target Cartwheel, and suggestions on how to maximize its adoption and effectiveness
- Designed a detailed PowerPoint presentation to re-brand Diet Coke as a "Smart Everyday Lifestyle Choice" for boomer and millennial consumers

**Leadership Experience:**

**Student International Business Council (SIBC) Project Leader**                                    **Summer 2015 - Present**
- Established a new partnership between the SIBC and Chick-fil-A, Inc. by leading a team of marketing students to research a project (pending) and present findings to representatives from Chick-fil-A, Inc. at their Headquarters in Atlanta, GA
- Introduced and independently led the first-ever Marketing Research and Analytics project to the SIBC and its members

**Student Union Board: Programmer**                                                             **Spring 2013 - Spring 2015**
- Earned profit for the Student Union Board on a majority of movie licenses purchased in Spring 2015 semester, averaging nearly $1000/movie in revenues
- Synthesized creative promotional plans to advertise upcoming events and movies to the student body
- Voted "Committee Member of the Month" by peers for exceptional commitment to the Student Union Board

**Fisher Hall Vice President**                                                                                  **Spring 2015**
- Reported weekly to the Hall Presidents' Council as a representative of Fisher Hall
- Planned and executed the "25th Annual" Fisher Regatta, which hosted hundreds of students from across campus

**Fisher Hall Freshman Orientation Staff**                                                          **Summer 2013 - Fall 2013**
- Assisted all incoming freshman during move-in and aid in their adjustment to life at Notre Dame
- Coordinated events and planned activities for over two thousand incoming freshmen, such as "Domerfest 2013"

**Additional Skills:** Proficient in Microsoft PowerPoint, Excel, Access and Word. Proficient in SPSS Statistical Software
**Languages:** English (Fluent), French (Conversational), "R" Statistical Software (Proficient)

## Resume 3

---

### JANET (JANE) MOLTON
Current Address: 123 Drury Lane | Bakerstown, IN 46637 | jmolton@nd.edu | (555) 222-1000|
Permanent Address: 20 Ginger Bread Trail|Joytown, PA 15821|

**EDUCATION**

| | | |
|---|---|---|
| **University of Notre Dame** | Notre Dame, IN | May 2016 |
| Bachelor of Business Administration | Major: Marketing | GPA: 3.54/4.0 |
| | Supplementary Minor: Journalism, Ethics, and Democracy | |

**HONORS**

· University of Notre Dame Dean's List—Fall 2012, Spring 2013, Spring 2015
· Target Corporation Case Study, Runner-up of "Happy and Healthy Guest" Campaign Project—Fall 2013

**EXPERIENCE**

| | | |
|---|---|---|
| **CBS News, London Bureau** | London, UK | Summer 2015 |
| *Intern* | | |

- Improved on-camera and writing skills by working with bureau correspondents to produce a news piece
- Learned camera practices by training with camera crews and assisting camera crews on live shoots and interviews
- Enhanced video editing techniques by logging various video and interview footage with Avid Media Composer
- Developed knowledge of production, edit, control and desk operations by working with producers on pieces from start to finish
- Worked with the news desk and producers on research and pitch projects and daily operations, like creating the daily paper trawl

| | | |
|---|---|---|
| **Cramer-Krasselt (C-K)** | Chicago, IL | Summer 2015 |
| *Public Relations Intern* | | |

- Expanded social media practices by helping lead community management across various clients' social media platforms
- Demonstrated social media knowledge by putting together client social reports and presenting the report on conference calls
- Enhanced pitch writing and media relations skills by pitching the C-K intern project and securing a placement in Agency Spy
- Improved writing as well as agency communication practices by writing agency blogs and employee biographies
- Developed event planning skills with a client's influencer event by compiling event briefing binders, putting together media and influencer lists, overseeing gift bag order and assembly, assisting at the event and creating social content and post-event reports

| | | |
|---|---|---|
| **Amy Levy Public Relations (ALPR)** | Los Angeles, CA | Summer 2014 |
| *Intern* | | |

- Learned social media techniques to increase outreach by running clients' accounts across various social media platforms
- Enhanced TV production and script-writing skills by outlining a client's segment for FOX Good Day LA
- Improved writing skills by managing clients' blogs, composing the ALPR newsletter and creating website content
- Demonstrated communicative skills by pitching media outlets to secure advertisements, story features, events and appearances

| | | |
|---|---|---|
| **The Observer Newspaper** | Notre Dame, IN | Fall 2012-Present |
| *Assistant Sports Editor, Production Assistant, Sports Reporter* | | |

- Developed writing skills by composing daily articles and editing peers' articles as Assistant Sports Editor
- Demonstrated media relations skills by conducting interviews with coaches and players, attending press conferences and coordinating with SIDs and the Notre Dame Media Relations staff
- Documented the seasons of Notre Dame athletic teams, including Football, Hockey, Men's Soccer, Men's Lacrosse, Men's Golf and Men's Boxing by writing features and articles
- Covered Notre Dame Men's Soccer team through its 2013 National Championship season via articles and social media
- Worked together with fellow staff under pressure and deadline to produce the daily paper

| | | |
|---|---|---|
| **NDtv** | Notre Dame, IN | Fall 2013-Present |
| *Host of Irish Insights Live, Sports Reporter and Anchor* | | |

- Developed on-camera skills with anchoring, interviewing and on-sight broadcasting
- Learned various production roles, including script-writing, teleprompter, camera and graphics techniques
- Demonstrated camera and editing skills by creating packages for episodes
- Expanded show outreach by promoting *Irish Insights Live* across social media platforms

**LEADERSHIP AND ACTIVITIES**

| | | |
|---|---|---|
| Teaching Assistant, Introduction to Marketing | Notre Dame, IN | Spring 2014-Present |

**SKILLS AND INTERESTS**

· *Computer*: Proficient in Avid Media Composer, ENPS, Final Cut Pro, Sysomos, Microsoft, InDesign, PhotoShop, Social Media, Cision

## Resume 4

# Carmen O'Brien

123 Drury Lane, Bakerstown, IN 46637
cobrien@nd.edu  |  (555) 222-1000

## Education

University of Notre Dame
Notre Dame, IN
BBA, Marketing, May 2014
Major GPA: 3.80/4.00
Cumulative GPA: 3.63/4.00
Dean's List: Fall 2011, Spring 2012,
Spring 2013

University of Notre Dame
London Program
London, England
International Studies, Spring 2013

## Coursework

Principles of Marketing, Consumer
Behavior, Marketing Research,
International Business Ethics, Public
Relations, Strategic Marketing,
Building Great Brands, Social Media,
Sports Marketing, Exploring Frontiers
of Marketing Thought, Graphic Design
1, Typography, Web Design

## Skills

Microsoft Office, Adobe Creative
Suite, Adobe Dreamweaver, Adobe
Fireworks, Adobe Muse, HTML/
CSS, Blogger, Tumblr, search engine
optimization, press release writing

## Experience

**TSA Communications**
Warsaw, IN
*Creative/PR Intern, Summer 2013*
- Designed print and web advertisements and company literature
- Performed search engine optimization for clients
- Wrote news releases and created email campaigns for clients

**Student International Business Council**
University of Notre Dame
*Researcher/Presenter, Fall 2011–Fall 2012*
- Participated in marketing-related projects for NBC Sports, Li-Ning and Target
- Researched and analyzed data and ideas and provided weekly input and a final individual report
- Traveled to Target and Acquity Group World Headquarters to present findings

**Martin's Supermarket**
Warsaw, IN
*Salad Bar, Summer 2011–Summer 2012*
- Kept salad bar stocked throughout the day and prepared food
- Monitored inventory of items and ingredients
- Closed and cleaned bar in a timely manner

**Principles of Marketing, 20100**
University of Notre Dame
*Team Co-Captain, Fall 2011*
- Managed a team of seven in completing semester-long project
- Used marketing techniques, primarily the Four Ps, to select a product and plan a product launch
- Compiled research and information into a 270-page professional report and presentation

## Resume 5

# ANGELA SCHAEFFER
Marketing | Social Media | Idea Generation

- 555.222.1000
- aschaeffer@yahoo.com
- www.aschaeffer.com

## // ABOUT ME

I have always loved the creative freedom of art ever since I was a small child, and I strive to apply that same passion to everything I do, big or small. As a marketing major with specializations in Social Media and Creative Idea Generation, I relish in the limitless bounds of potential that these fields can provide. It gives me a chance to apply my imagination to projects that inspire and motivate me. The chance to have an impact drives me to provide the most innovative and transformative handiwork I can produce, and provide a tangible difference for those I am working for.

## // EXPERIENCE

### MARKETING INTERN @HomeAid Sacramento
JUNE 2015 - PRESENT

I hold a great many causes near to my heart, so I relish in my job working with a nonprofit. It is a hands on working environment, where I am currently working on social media efforts, website development and consulting, and market research.

### MARKETING INTERN @Lionakis
MAY 2015 - AUG 2015

This internship was a unique experience to take a look into a world of marketing few know about. I assisted in a variety of tasks, including PR, social media consulting and blogging, and development of their proposal for Firm of the Year with the California State AIA.

### INTERN @ConnectIreland
SUMMER 2014

As a student at ND and a U.S. citizen, I was in a unique position to assist ConnectIreland in their efforts. I assisted in finding new connections, marketing the company to potential new clients, website development, and finding sustainable new ways to improve their unique business model, while gaining experience in an unfamiliar place.

## // INTERESTS

COOKING | CREATIVE WRITING | TRAVELING | READING | NETWORKING

## // SKILLS

IDEA GENERATION
PUBLIC SPEAKING
SOCIAL MEDIA
PR

## // EDUCATION

### UNIVERSITY OF NOTRE DAME
2012-CURRENT

Marketing Major in the Mendoza School of Business, and Italian Minor

### ST. FRANCIS HIGH SCHOOL
2008-2012

Debate and Speech Captain
Champion in Speech and Debate

### LANGUAGES

ENGLISH *(FLUENT)*
ITALIAN *(SEMIFLUENT)*

## // REFERRALS

### JANE RANG
Executive Director
HomeAid Sacramento
Jane@homeaidsac.org

### LUKE NOON
Principal
Lionakis
Luke.Noon@lionakis.com

### GEORGE TALVERN
Head of Operations
ConnectIreland
gtalvern@connectireland.com

## Resume 6

*Change is inevitable, progress is optional*

# Corinne Zaidel

123 Drury Lane ● Bakerstown, IN 46637 ● Phone: 1-555-222-1000 ● E-Mail: czaidel@nd.edu

**Education**     **Work Experience & Leadership**     **Volunteer**     **Skills**

**University of Notre Dame**

    Business
    Concentration: Marketing
    GPA: 3.615/4.0
    Present-May 2016
    Dean's List: Fall 2012,

**University of Notre Dame Australia**

    Business
    Concentration: Marketing
    Fremantle, AU
    July 2014 – November 2014

**University College Dublin**

    Irish literature and history
    Dublin, Ireland
    May 2013 - July 2013

**Special Olympics Notre Dame (SOND)**

- Participation in Breaking Barriers Fashion Show and SOND events to raise awareness and funds for individuals with disabilities

**College Mentor For Kids**

- Mentored a 4th grade student from South Bend by leading activities focused on engagement and higher education benefits

**Social Concerns Seminar: Appalachia**

- Introduced to the social and cultural issues of the Appalachia region and worked hand-in-hand with the Hurley community in construction activities to improve the living conditions of individuals community members

- Bungee jumping
- Juggling
- Notre Dame club soccer
- Racquet ball
- Sports enthusiast
- World traveler
- Demonstrates in depth knowledge of Microsoft Office: Excel, Access, PowerPoint, Word
- Adept at creating and delivering oral presentations
- Sarcasm

**Fiat Chrysler Automobiles Multicultural Marketing Intern**          May 2015 – August 2015

- Developed the 2016 Multicultural Marketing Plan for Chrysler, Jeep, Dodge, Ram & FIAT brands to reach U.S multicultural consumers, which are 85% of the U.S population growth in the last decade and 62% of automotive industry growth, through data and market analysis
- Assisted with creative concepts, production planning and post-production for the 2015 Chrysler 200, Ram 1500 and Dodge Family Hispanic Tier I advertising campaigns
- In deep communications with our advertising agency, brand teams, and regional business centers to expand our campaigns beyond advertising to dealer activations, celebrity partnerships, philanthropic opportunities, public relations, event sponsorships, and social media

**Student Manager Notre Dame Phone Center**          Jan 2013 – Currently employed

- Using communication, problem-solving and leadership skills to supervise students calling Alumni to raise donations for the university

**Unleashed Notre Dame**          Spring 2015

- Lead social enterprise consultant for a start up company that encourages the independence of Nicaraguan women and boosts the local economy; responsible for business models, market research, impact measurement, sustainability and brand imaging in a team

**Vivint Sales Representative**          May 2014 - July 2014

- Outside sales representative responsible for selling personalized home automation and security systems directly to customers

**Student International Business Council**          Fall 2012 - Spring 2014

- Co-leader of the HealthScape consulting case working with specific companies to navigate the changing healthcare landscape
- Development of quantitative data and marketing techniques for Under Armour and Groupon in selective McKinsey & Company cases

## Resume 7

### Kara Johnson

**contact.**

555.222.1000   sarajohnson@aol.com   linkedin.com/sarajohnson

**education.**

**University of Notre Dame May 2014** | Marketing & Graphic Design
Bachelors degrees in Marketing & Design
**Dublin Jerome High School Class of 2010** | Valedictorian
International Baccalaureate Diploma

**skills.**

Id   Ai   Ps   Lr   Fl   Dw   W   X   O   P

InDesign   Illustrator   Photoshop   Lightroom   Flash   Dreamweaver   Word   Excel   Outlook   PowerPoint

**experience.**

**Ryan Hall** | Resident Assistant
*August 2013 - Present*
- Facilitated conflict resolution among residents
- Developed a positive living environment within the hall

**Draftfcb** | Account Management Intern
*Summer 2013*
- Assisted the Account Executive in the management of Nestle's Tombstone and DiGiorno's pizza brands
- Researched and presented competitive insights report utilized by Nestle Account team
- Winner of Intern Blackhawk Ticket pitch
- Winner of 2013 Intern Think Tank challenge

**Notre Dame RecSports** | Designer
*November 2012 - May 2013*
- Designed posters and other marketing materials for campus recreational sports department
- Managed and upgraded web-based content for fitness classes using Conductor

**Business Foresight** | Teaching Assistant
*December 2012 - May 2013*
- Resource for semester-long research project concerning global implications in business

**Student International Business Council** | Team Lead
*2010 - December 2012*
- Investigated capturing urban markets for Target
- Strategized how to increase site traffic for PEPY rides by employing Google AdWords
- Selected to present "Red vs. Black" advertising campaign to Coca-Cola in Cincinnati, OH
- Led 20 students in the analysis of Li-Ning case study for the Fall 2012 semester

**Marathon Petroleum Corp.** | Brand Marketing Intern
*Summer 2012*
- Designed sales analysis templates with company Online Analytical Processing (OLAP) cubes
- Discussed market intelligence and strategies with contracted wholesalers
- Helped facilitate company hosting of FPMA Trade Show in Orlando, FL

**BRC Printing Company** | Intern
*Summer 2011*
- Collected and analyzed nationwide early education standardized test scores
- Created a cohesive report utilized by government officials and the Belizean Ministry of Education

**numbers.**

 half and full marathons completed **6**

 times eaten mac and cheese **0**

faces painted at the Columbus Zoo **432**

 nights spent in a Latin American convent **39**

**activities.**

**Notre Dame Women's Boxing** | Competitive Boxer, Captain | September 2011 - Present
- Participated in charity boxing tournament raising over $25,000 for schools in Uganda, Africa
- Organized and designed fundraising poster and photoshoot contributing to highest to date attendance

**South Bend Police Department Boxing Club** | Volunteer | May 2011 - Present
- Taught basic boxing skills to community youth ranging in ages from seven to eighteen

**The Observer** | Photographer, Multimedia Editor | 2010 - August 2013
- Captured various campus events to be featured in daily newspaper
- Coordinated the layout and editing of relevant photos to be printed and viewed online

# RESUME CONTENT

## Quantify accomplishments.[3]

Quite simply, numbers are convincing. On your resume, try to quantify as many of your accomplishments as you can. Numbers and related quantitative improvements provide recruiters with a much better feel for the real impact you had in any particular line item. For example, which internship experience description sounds better to you?

- ❖ **Intern 1:** Duties included taking field measurements and maintaining records, setting up and tracking project using Microsoft Project, and developing computerized materials sheets.
- ❖ **Intern 2:** Initiated and managed tracking systems used for the Green District water decontamination project, helped to save more than $45,000 on the overall project through a 30% decrease of staff allocation time.

Those two line items describe the exact same experience, but the second one is much more eye catching and impressive. Use numbers wherever they make sense.

But what if you didn't really work with hard numbers in your internship, club, or some other accomplishment described on your resume? With some creative thinking, you can still generally add some numbers for many items on your resume—even those involving primarily softer skills and experiences. There are different ways to try to quantify specific experiences. Let's consider a couple of these.[4]

## Estimate ranges.

Not knowing the exact figure for things is often a big deterrent to students for trying to use numbers in their resumes. One way to overcome this is to use a range. It is okay to not know the exact initial benchmark or exactly how many of this or that you worked with. That doesn't mean you shouldn't still try to quantify it. Give it your best estimate for more impact. Which description sounds more impressive to you?

- ❖ **Before:** Tutored engineering students in Calculus.
- ❖ **After:** As a University tutor, I worked with six to 10 engineering students each term during my last four semesters. These students initially failed the calculus course requirement. All but three of the 30 plus students I tutored eventually passed the requirement and are now on-schedule to graduate in four years with their engineering degrees in hand.

## Include frequency.

Another way to add some numbers into your resume is to include how frequently you did a particular task. This is particularly helpful in illustrating your work in high-volume situations—a hiring manager will be able to see just how much you can handle.

❖ **Before:** Helped my marketing professor as a research assistant.
❖ **After:** Reviewed and pre-screened an average of 10 new article submissions per week for my professor, the editor of *XYZ Marketing Journal*. My recommendations on which should be included or excluded helped my professor and her editorial to team reduce the average review time by nearly 40 percent during my year and a half in this position.

## Note the scale.

Employers love to save money—and recruiters are always impressed by resumes that include energetic, innovative efforts to do just that. Review what you did during your internship. How often did you perform and re-perform a duty that helped to improve the bottom line? Such tasks might have included a host of different potential roles you performed—for example, streamlining a procedure, saving time for someone else so they could dedicate more time to their primary role, or fulfilling other responsibilities that reduced costs or enhanced revenue. How often did you do this? How much time did you save? What specific costs did you reduce and by how much? Even rough estimates will help.[5]

❖ **Before:** Summer internship with an auto loan processing company. Job involved making copies of loan files. Helped to streamline to filing process.
❖ **After:** Redesigned auto loan file process, increasing efficiency by 50% and generating an annual savings of $70,000 per year.

❖ **Before:** Chaired the Student Event Promotional Committee.
❖ **After:** Chaired promotional committee of 12 and presented marketing plans to 40 to 60 students at weekly university senate meetings open to all 2,000 community members.

In sum, numbers make a big difference in resumes, no matter what your work involves. So try adding a few numbers to quantify your work and see how they help to drive home the impacts you have made.

# Include your GPA and other quantifiable indicators of superior academic achievements.

## To include your GPA or not?

That is the question. The default answer is: when in doubt, do include your GPA on your resume. A number of factors may come into play as you consider whether or not to include your GPA on your resume. These include variables such as:

❖ What is your GPA? (The higher, the more appropriate it is to include, especially if you are applying for your first full-time position.);
❖ From what college or university did you receive your degree? (A lower GPA from Harvard is more noteworthy than a lower GPA from a small community college.);

❖ In what specific discipline is your degree? (A lower GPA in physics or mathematics stands out more than the same GPA in a softer science);

❖ Is your marketing (or related) GPA higher than your cumulative GPA? (If so, and if your marketing GPA is considerably higher than your overall GPA, then consider separating out your that marketing GPA.)

❖ Will this be your first full-time job after graduation? (If so, including your GPA is more relevant than it would be if this is not your first job.); and

❖ For what type of marketing position are you applying?

Next we discuss some of these and other potentially relevant factors to consider when deciding whether or not to include your GPA on your resume.

## GPA is often an important initial screening device.

For some more competitive positions, a recruiter or HR staffer might be faced with the challenge of reviewing a large stack of resumes. In such situations, GPA is often one of the most important initial screening criterions. As a new college grad seeking a competitive position, therefore, not including your GPA in your resume can be a red flag, immediately and automatically precluding you from consideration for many available marketing positions. How many positions? A reasonable estimate would be 70% to 90% or more, depending on the nature, requirements, and number of candidates competing for any specific position.

## Will this be your first full-time job after graduation?

Once you have proven yourself in the marketplace for a few years, your next resume will focus on your accomplishments since college. From that point forward, therefore, you can certainly exclude your GPA from your resume without adverse effect for most, but not all, areas of marketing. For example, Google and some other high tech companies, when filling positions demanding intellectual rigor, may ask for a transcript even from those candidates 2 to 4 years out of college as an early step in the application process.

## For what type of marketing position are you applying?

Recruiters for some positions (e.g., marketing research or market data analytics) will only consider candidates who have proven their intellectual capacity and discipline through excellent academic performance. These recruiters comb their stacks of resumes, pulling out for careful consideration only students with GPAs of 3.5 or higher, depending upon the academic reputation of the degree-granting university or college. This does not mean that a student with a 3.0 GPA cannot succeed in a position demanding high intellectual acumen, but the prospects for success for lower GPA students are relatively low versus the prospects for higher GPA students. Thus, given a large stack of resumes, it is simply more efficient for the recruiter to automatically eliminate lower GPA candidates from careful consideration for certain positions.

## What if you have a low GPA?

Recruiters for some other positions (e.g., many sales representatives and customer service employees) are often comfortable with candidates with a lower GPA (3.0 or under—perhaps as low as 2.2 or 2.3, depending on the school). But this is only the case if the candidate can use her/his resume, leadership stories (see below), and interview skills to evidence much sought-after traits such as a strong work ethic, time management skills, leadership experiences, a drive to compete and win, and proven measured success in other skill areas that might be particularly relevant for any specific position. Demonstrating those highly valued traits is a must for low GPA students, but can be particularly challenging to communicate effectively and convincingly in a resume alone. That is why we highly recommend always complementing one's resume with a battery of relevant "leadership stories" (our next topic). [6] These are important for all students, but may be particularly important for students with lower GPAs.

# What about high school standout accomplishments?

Our presumption in this book is that you are about 22 years old, having graduated from high school between four and five years ago. That is not too long ago. So, what about all that hard work and those standout awards and recognition you earned in your high school days? Here are some general principles to follow.

❖ If you have significant, standout, measureable achievements from college, your outstanding accomplishments from high school are typically not needed or appropriate for your entry-level, post-college resume.

❖ That said, in both academics and athletics in particular, it can be much more difficult to stand out in college than in high school. You want your resume to include clearly visible proofs of qualities highly valued by recruiters—qualities such as intellect, discipline, energy, commitment, passion, competitiveness, a strong work ethic, teamwork, and other leadership skills. If some of your personal best proofs of such key differentiators are not from the ultra-competitive environment you faced in college but from your high school days, we suggest you do include highlights of your most outstanding high school accomplishments on your entry-level resume.

❖ Were you a top high school student? Indicate a measure of that (GPA, class rank, National Honor Society, etc.). Were you a class officer? What office(s) did you hold and for how long? What did you change and improve at your school? Did you start or lead a club? Were you a competitive athlete with awards and acknowledgements? Indicate these successes and some measure of what you accomplished.

Again, these do not belong front and center, and should be omitted altogether if you have achieved similar standout distinctions in college. But even if not needed to beef up your post-college entry-level resume, some of your truly outstanding high school accomplishments might provide the best proofs you have of some of the attributes you want to express. So, do not automatically dismiss the idea of including high school accomplishments somewhere in your materials.

# RESUME LENGTH

## How long should your resume be?

*Bottom line first*. A "one- page rule" applies for the vast majority of new college grads seeking an entry-level position.

"How long should my resume be?" is one of the most commonly asked questions about resumes. Not too long ago, job seekers were told that a resume should never exceed one page. That is still relevant for most new college graduates. Resumes of those new graduates who break this 'this golden rule' may be immediately destined for the circular file – i.e., the waste basket.

As your career evolves and matures, however, that old 'golden rule' will no longer hold. Times have changed, and so has the criteria for resume length. The new guideline is: A resume should be long enough to entice hiring managers to call you for job interviews. That may sound vague, but there is no hard-and-fast resume length rule that works for everyone. Factors to consider in determining the appropriate length of your resume include career objective, occupation, industry, years of experience, number of employers in your history, scope of accomplishments and education/training.

Before presenting some general thoughts on when a resume length of one page, two page, or three page of more is appropriate, here are some other factors that should come into play as you deliberate about the appropriate length of your own resume.

- ❖ Your resume is a career-marketing tool, not an autobiography. Strive to keep your resume concise and focused on your key selling points. *Let go of past experiences that do not market you for your current goal. Every word in the resume should sell your credentials and value to a potential employer.*

- ❖ *You want to leave something fresh and substantial to talk about in your interviews.*

- ❖ It is common for employers or recruiters to sort through hundreds, or even thousands, of resumes to fill one position. Hiring managers often give resumes just a cursory glance before deciding if the applicant deserves to be added to the "maybe" pile. While your resume will probably get a more thorough read if you are called for a job interview, *ensure that your strongest selling points are immediately* and *highly visible to the reviewer. This argues for a short, concise, well-focused resume full of hard hitting bullets right at the start of each section.*

## Use a one-page resume if:

❖ You have fewer than 10 years of experience.
❖ You are pursuing a radical career change, and most of your experience is not relevant to your new goal.
❖ You have held only one or two positions with one employer.

*This "one- page rule" applies for the vast majority of new college grads seeking an entry-level position.*

## Use a two-page resume if:

❖ You have 10 or more years of experience related to your goal.
❖ Your field requires technical or engineering skills, and you need space to list and prove your technical knowledge.

Put the most important information at the top of the first page. Lead your resume with a career summary so your key credentials appear at the forefront. On the second page, include a page number, your name, and contact information.

## Consider a three-page resume or longer if:

❖ You are a senior-level manager or executive with a long track record of leadership accomplishments.
❖ You are in an academic or scientific field with extensive publications, speaking engagements, professional courses, licenses, or patents. An academic resume may be 20 pages or longer.

Multiple-page resumes can use addenda after page two. Job seekers can decide whether to send the full document or just the first two pages to a potential employer, based on the job opportunity requirements.[7]

# ADDING TO AND EXPANDING YOUR RESUME

## Enhance your background over time.

If you have identified a dream marketing career path but feel that you presently come up short on the required education, experiences, and general background, it is never too late to remedy that by enhancing your background and battery of experiences, thereby enhancing your resume. This is particularly true for college students and recent graduates.

### Document your experiences in a portfolio.

First of all, recognize that you likely already have more background than immediately comes to mind. Document your many and varied learning experiences by starting a portfolio to evidence this background to prospective employers. For example, include items such as the following:

❖ *Individual course projects.* Describe the motivation, approach, content, and result of specific research- and writing-related projects and papers you have completed.

❖ *Team course projects.* Again, describe the motivation, approach, content, and result. Focus on relating your role as an integral part of the team—avoiding the temptation to take credit for organizing and running the whole project.

❖ *Club projects and activities.* What was the project motivation, approach, content and result? What specific role did you play? What did you actually do? How did you handle non-optimal results (e.g., perhaps few members came to an event) and then collaborate with other club leaders to improve the results the next time? Include metrics if relevant—for example, how many club members and others participated? Compare your results to a previous benchmark. What did you learn from this experience?

❖ *Part time jobs while at school.* Positive job experiences and related evidence speak to your work ethic, commitment, discipline, ability to work independently, and time-management skills. How many hours? What were you doing? How did you balance work and school responsibilities?

❖ *Summer internships.* A story about any summer internship provides an opportunity for you to describe and prove: your discipline in meeting regular work hours consistently; your work ethic; and your tenacity. If you became passionate about any particular dimension of the internship experience, describe the "what" and "why" of that enthusiasm. Prospective employers love young folks who show passion and enthusiasm about virtually anything. If you interned in some area of marketing, so much the better.

## Take some online courses.

Quality online courses are readily available in nearly any area to help you start filling any educational gaps. For example, a recent survey in the area of digital marketing revealed that only a small fraction of those with burgeoning digital careers actually had any formal education whatsoever in digital marketing.[8] Search for tips on building background and gaining experience in new areas of marketing on sites and videos like "How to Get a Job in Digital Marketing."[9]

## Start and lead a club.

Take the lead in gathering together a team to start a club and try to make it flourish. Build an online presence using multiple social platforms to expand and enhance the club's membership.

The club does not have to solve world problems—start a Left-handers' club, a turtle club, a ballroom dance club, a cooking club, a pottery club, a fly-fishing club, a fan club for some under-appreciated sport at your college or university—a club about any passion you may have. Use your imagination.

Set up an informal structure. Plan and implement regular activities to expand their scope and your club's visibility over time. Document your activities and plot the growth of membership and participation.

Indicating in your resume that you have started a club from scratch, grown it significantly, and run it successfully helps recruiters infer several positive traits:

* ❖ You are a self-starter, full of the passion, ambition, drive, creativity, and tenacity, in addition to the ability to rally others toward a common cause;
* ❖ You are willing to tackle something new. You are unafraid of the inherent risks of being unsuccessful in a new venture or simply being wrong in any, perhaps many, dimensions of the venture;
* ❖ You are an organized planner who envisions unforeseen events and has contingency plans ready to go;
* ❖ You are a collaborator who possesses the leadership and social skills necessary to gather and motivate your officer team to enthusiastically and cooperatively help with creative planning. You are willing both to volunteer and follow through on designing and implementing club events and initiatives.
* ❖ You radiate self-confidence and have had enough successful leadership experiences in your background to be comfortable driving forward into virtually any new territory, facing any new challenge, without a blueprint or having someone guide you step by step. You do not have to be told or shown exactly how to do something that is new to you—in fact, you have the curiosity, energy, intellect, and determination to learn how to do new things. You have successfully tackled new challenges and undertaken new ventures in the past and know that you can do so again and again in the future. You actively and willingly access the expertise of fellow club members or other resources to succeed in new endeavors.
* ❖ You follow through, despite the inevitable wrong turn here and there. Ultimately, you are committed to completing the challenges you undertake— and completing them well.

Thus, starting and successfully running a new club broadcasts to recruiters your energy, imagination, tenacity, discipline, strong work ethic, resiliency, teamwork, and other visible leadership skills that are in high demand by most employers. Furthermore, you can use this experience to generate multiple leadership stories (described in the next section) to evidence your readiness for nearly any desired marketing career. In sum, you can reap huge career benefits by starting and running your own club.

## Finally, always keep your resume updated.[10]

Once you land that first position, it's easy to let your resume grow old and out of date with your accomplishments. The same holds true for your LinkedIn profile—many recent grads neglect this important professional presence. The temptation is clear: If you are not planning on searching for a new position anytime soon, why spend the time and trouble to regularly update your profiles?

As you review the reasons presented below for keeping your documentation up to date, keep in mind that this is all about you—it is your life and career. Updating your resume doesn't have to take a huge amount of time, especially if you're doing it regularly. Carving out 30 minutes every month to keep your resume current can pay big dividends indeed. Consider these motivating reasons to spend that time:

## Be ready for promotion opportunities.

Even if you love your entry-level position, eventually you'll look to start moving up the ladder. When a job opens up, even though your direct manager knows your outstanding capabilities and might recommend you, the higher-ups will still want to see your profile, qualifications, experience, and accomplishments on paper. Will you be ready? Or will one of your parallel colleagues get the position because her or his materials were updated and ready to view?

By having a current resume on hand, readily available to anyone, you'll be able to respond to inquiries of interest from top management immediately, with no need to stress out while hurriedly working to bring your materials up-to-date to present yourself in the best light. Another advantage is that having your materials ready to go at all times will demonstrate not only your suitability for a relevant, potential elevated position, but also your enthusiasm for pursuing the promotion.

## Keep yourself professionally mobile, pursuing that dream opportunity at a moment's notice.

Just because you're not looking for a new job doesn't mean someone else isn't looking for someone exactly like you. Recruiters always keep an eye out for the perfect fit. If they come across your three-year-old resume or LinkedIn profile, they're unlikely to be impressed.

But what if they see an up-to-date resume or profile detailing all of the impressive things you've done recently? They might just extend you an offer that you'd have a hard time turning down (and, at the very least, it'll be a nice confidence boost!).

## Prepare an immediate response for unexpected lay-offs.

Unfortunately, no matter how much you love your job or how stellar you perform, mergers, cutbacks, economic downturns, new partnerships and a host of other situations can result in your getting laid off unexpectedly. When that happens, you're going to have enough to think about without throwing your ancient resume into the mix. Updating your credentials even when you're not looking for a job will keep you from overlooking new experiences, areas of expertise, and related achievements. But just as importantly, you will be only a few contacts and a cover letter away from immediately bouncing back into the job market.[11]

## Build your reputation as an expert.

Getting invitations to speak at conferences, write short articles, or provide quotes to key media outlets in your area of expertise can help you grow professionally without leaving your current position. To pitch yourself to the media or conference organizers and make yourself credible, you have to be immediately ready with your updated resume, enhanced with the recent experiences you've gained not only through your day-to-day position, but also through your presentations, articles, quotes, etc. In other words, you should demonstrate your ongoing participation in conferences and involvement with media.

## Stay current in case someone wants to nominate or recognize you for your performance.

If you have been performing extremely well at work and/or in a leadership role for a professional organization, professional superiors or colleagues might ask to nominate you for special recognition. Regardless of how stellar your performance has been, the accolade will likely require verification of your suitability. Such recognition creates a special opportunity for you—one in which you should be glowing with satisfaction, not hustling to collect documentation of the very performance for which you are to be nominated. In catch-up mode, you might not truly reflect the depth or breadth of your true accomplishments in your rushed resume update. The strain could leave you hassled and frustrated and your generous nominators potentially embarrassed. This suboptimal situation is one you can easily avoid by devoting 30 minutes or so every month to maintaining your resume. Ultimately, it's your life. It is your career. It is your resume. Why not keep it up to date?

# LEADERSHIP STORIES

# PURPOSE

## What are leadership stories?[12]

We highly recommend that you spend considerable effort developing a number of personal "leadership stories." You will use these stories to expand upon and testify to the skills, experiences and related accomplishments that are listed only briefly on your resume.

Your leadership stories should flow from your internship experiences and from prior personal, academic, athletic, social, club, dorm, and volunteer activities—any successes that speak to your leadership skills and related attributes. By elaborating on your achievements, you not only make the resume line items easier to understand, but you also provide recruiters with a stronger feel for the traits you exemplified and proved through those accomplishments.

## How you can use your leadership stories?

Your leadership stories and your ability to tell them with enthusiasm will be invaluable assets in the search for an attractive marketing position. Consider the two primary uses of your stories:

- ❖ Stories as a resume attachment. Your stories make a logical complement and excellent potential addendum to your resume for any job application.
- ❖ Stories help you stand out in your interviews. Your stories provide the substance for any interview situation you will be facing—whether on the phone, via Skype or FaceTime, or face-to-face.

Your stories will be particularly valuable when you are invited for on-site, face-to-face interviews with prospective employers. In these situations, you might speak with many different people for a half-day or more. Your stories will provide quality content that you can immediately recall to answer standard introductory questions such as, "Tell me about yourself" or "Walk me through your resume," by interviewers who may or may not have done their homework on you.

These are *your* stories—as such, they provide a prime opportunity to show:

- ❖ Your self-confidence, maturity, and general communication skills;
- ❖ Your personal and social skills; and, perhaps most importantly,
- ❖ Your passion and enthusiasm. After all, if you can't get passionate when talking about your proudest moments, then what is the interviewer to conclude about your ability to become passionate about anything?

Furthermore, your stories can also benefit your recommenders. Sharing stories with your references helps them write stellar letters for you that integrate very specific, credible, and influential comments about your unique qualifications.

# CONTENT

## What sources should you use?

Include experiences from your internship(s) and from your past personal (college and high school) challenges and successes related to academics, sports, social activities, clubs, dorm life, or volunteer activities—any areas where you have exhibited leadership and related attributes.

As cautioned earlier in Step 2, when using team projects, don't pretend you did it all—employers know you did not. Instead, point out your personal contributions and any areas in which you led your team in successfully addressing relevant challenges.

The stories do not all have to be about changing the world. In fact, one favorite "determination" story concerns how a student was able – only with considerable effort - to get one of the dining halls at Notre Dame bring back Quaker Oatmeal Squares. (This particular story is included in the examples below, and testifies to student's determination, commitment and grit to right something she felt was wrong – no matter how inconsequential in the big scheme of things.)

## Broaden the topics for your leadership stories.

Below we provide a long list of personal and professional attributes that most recruiters value in their search for the next great employee.

While no two prospective positions require the same exact set of superior attributes, there is a great deal of overlap. Projected performance in most positions is enhanced by proven qualities such as those listed below.

No one possesses all of these generally desirable qualities. But the more that you have and, particularly, the more that you can evidence with your stories, the more attractive your package and you will be for prospective employers.

## Highly valued attitudes and attributes (in no particular order) include:

- ❖ Passion and enthusiasm—about anything and everything
- ❖ High energy and a strong work ethic
- ❖ Strong social skills, with a friendly, engaging personality and high comfort level in new social situations
- ❖ Superior personal and professional communication skills—written, verbal, and presentation
- ❖ Maturity—your readiness and willingness to take charge, plan, organize, lead, and follow through
- ❖ Natural leadership and personal skills for gathering, attracting, rallying, and continually motivating colleagues
- ❖ Ability and desire to organize time and resources when necessary to get assigned tasks done well and on time
- ❖ A can-do, positive attitude about work and life in general
- ❖ Discipline, proven over and over again in your resume and stories
- ❖ Competitiveness and a drive to succeed and excel in any endeavor
- ❖ Time management and multi-tasking capabilities—the ability to juggle multiple activities simultaneously with some ease.
- ❖ You can meet deadlines without reminders or prodding.
- ❖ Tenacity with a committed drive to complete tasks undertaken
- ❖ Being a self-starter with the ability to identify and unite others toward a common cause
- ❖ Imagination and creativity – a willingness and ability to think outside of the box and challenge the status quo
- ❖ Curiosity and love of learning new things, with openness to new ideas and constant efforts to develop new skills
- ❖ Willingness and self-confidence to tackle new, heretofore unfamiliar challenges, and being unafraid of making mistakes

- Service-oriented, selfless concern for others and a ready willingness to commit time and energy to help
- Ability to work effectively independently and as part of a team
- Team-player mentality to embrace and enjoy working with any group or any type of people
- Willingness to take the lead in any group situation
- Resiliency and ability to handle, bounce back, and learn from failures and to channel rejection constructively
- Proven analytical skills—as/if relevant for the desired position.
- Detail-oriented mentality
- Comfort with all dimensions of Microsoft Office—particularly Excel, as a high proportion of marketing positions today require regular use of Excel
- Acknowledgement of shortcomings and active efforts to improve
- Specific capabilities unique to your potential field or position
- Foreign language skills
- Intercultural background and experiences
- Design, art, and/or graphics experiences
- Advanced analytical skills

To *help you jumpstart the process of developing your own stories, included below the next section are a number of leadership story examples that evidence some of the attributes listed above.*

# STRUCTURE

## How many stories?

Try to write a dozen or more stories if at all possible. Short stories are fine. To be done effectively, this will take you some time and effort. Take your time. Think about it. Jot down ideas on your smart phone or a note pad in your free time.

## How long should each story be?

Any length is fine. The examples include both short and long stories.

**Short Stories.** For each short story, focus on one or two of your specific strengths (with an example) that make you an attractive potential hire. Use one or two traits as the title to each short story and then give a quick example.

**Longer Stories.** Think about the following points for longer leadership stories:

- The situation when you arrived and the issues to be examined;
- The tasks you figured out needed to be done;
- The steps you took to address those issues, including getting others to assist or participate to leverage your own initiative and energy;
- The obstacles you and/or your team ran into and how you overcame them;
- The final result; and

❖ The leadership lesson(s) you learned from that experience and/or all your experiences taken together.

## How should you title your stories?

Put a small header or title before each story, whether short or long. The header should specifically list the attribute(s) that particular story demonstrates. Later on we will talk about changing title of any given story to focus on one or more traits most relevant for a specific target position and company.

# EXAMPLES OF LEADERSHIP STORIES

## Work ethic and time-management skills

Looking back now as a senior [xyz sport] player here at Notre Dame, one could say my career on the court has been somewhat rough. Four straight losing seasons made staying motivated extremely difficult for the whole team. Nevertheless, I can say that I did it—I maintained my commitment and enthusiasm throughout my entire time here. We trained up to 25 hours a week—not including the many hours per week required to prepare for and attend a full load of classes. Even the off-season could be exhausting, as we continued our training year round, getting up at 5 a.m. three times per week to work out and practice. The rigorous schedule has certainly frustrated my teammates and me at times, especially when the previous seasons had yielded little success, but both my teammates and I take pride in having stuck with it enthusiastically for all four years.

## Openness to learning new things

In summer 2014, I had the opportunity to work at a company in Italy for a month. Upon receiving the offer, I immediately began researching more about the country and language. I love Romance languages and seized the opportunity to learn another one so, before heading across the Atlantic; I bought the first round of Rosetta Stone to prepare. While in Italy, all of my co-workers kindly helped teach me various words, phrases, and grammar rules in Italian. They all noted how much of the language I was able to pick up in my short time there. I was not afraid to immerse myself in the culture, ask questions, and attempt to speak the language (even though I knew my grammar would be poor and my accent would be worse). Although I probably won't use Italian too much throughout my life, I relished the chance to learn a new skill and expand my knowledge.

## Love of taking on new challenges

For the past two and a half years, I have worked at the Notre Dame Development Phone Center. At first, my work consisted of calling alumni, family, and friends of the University to raise funds and build relationships. After three successful semesters of calling, I was promoted to student manager as a junior. I now lead a team of more than 100 student callers and manage operations of the Phone Center. I also lead "External Sales," through which I reach out to South Bend businesses and request gift cards or coupons as incentives for callers to perform well. In return, these businesses gain awareness on campus.

Before my promotion, the incentives system worked like this: callers received "points" through a complicated equation that factored in several components of their performance. They did not know exactly how points were earned. At the semester's end, callers redeemed points for gift cards and coupons via an auction.

As manager and leader of the External Sales operation, I realized the callers did not see any intrinsic link between their performance and the prizes they received later, at the end of the semester. Further, the cool prizes we tried so hard to get essentially functioned as bonuses, rather than motivation. Recognizing this problem, I strived this year to make the incentives system more incentivizing.

The callers now have full awareness of how to earn points thanks to heightened transparency, as well as a simplified commission-style system. They can also redeem points at any time during the semester, which fosters a healthy level of competition and a more direct and timely reward for good performance. Although the system is new this semester, I trust that the Phone Center will be both more productive and more fun based on my work.

## Passion and enthusiasm

On September 10, 20XX, I went to the Notre Dame football game against Michigan in Ann Arbor—a football game that changed my life. That may sound somewhat extreme, but the realization I had while at that game propelled me to pursue a project that would forever made a difference for the rest of my time at Notre Dame.

The atmosphere in the Big House blew me away. The fans fully engaged in the game, standing for every play and staying loud the entire time. Their unifying initiatives, from the color everyone wore to the pom-poms they waved and the music they played over the loudspeaker, created a truly electric atmosphere. Never wanting to give Michigan credit, I began to ask myself why Notre Dame's football atmosphere wasn't like that. I saw an opportunity for the Notre Dame football game experience to improve, and I took initiative to make that happen.

First, I looked to find a dedicated partner to work with me in realizing this vision. Together, we started setting up meetings with everyone who would listen to our ideas—athletic department employees, gameday operations, and marketing professors. We also conducted a student survey, collecting more than 800 responses gauging opinions on the current atmosphere and strategies to grow and improve. Our energy and thoughtfulness impressed the athletic department employees, who asked us what they could do to improve the atmosphere by the next home game. Our response was music in the stadium. They agreed.

Throughout the process, we received both positive and negative feedback. The main obstacle was the perception that we would change Notre Dame football, a tradition many see as timeless and untouchable. It was crucial for us to convey that adding music would not ruin the tradition of Notre Dame football; instead, we wanted to add more traditions and enhance the atmosphere. Notre Dame risked becoming a fatigued brand if we did not become more dynamic.

The final result of the project was playing recorded music in the stadium for the first time in Notre Dame history. It was an incredible feeling to have made such a difference and see that what started as a small idea grow into a full project.

As a leader, I realized problems only signal new opportunities. I also learned the importance of being persistent and standing up for what I believe in spite of dissenting opinions. I had data from the student survey and other schools to back up my reasoning, which helped my cause.

This project led me to craft an independent research class in fall 2012. Guided by a marketing professor, the "Gameday Guru" study let students visit other schools to evaluate what components contribute to the best football stadium atmosphere.

## Creative thinking

Last summer, I interned at Target in Minneapolis. The company's very well-established and well-organized intern program includes a kickball league made up of 12 different teams of interns. When my team came together to play our first game, I noticed that even with our excitement and passion, we blended in with the other teams. I realized we were missing something—uniforms.

That's when I came up with the idea to special order tank tops from a website that had our team name and a funny phrase on the back. I emailed my team, got the general consensus that my teammates agreed with me, and designed a shirt myself. I then paid for the entire order and was able to collect the appropriate amount form every member of the team.

When shirts arrived the following week and we showed up in our matching uniforms, the other kickball teams grew slightly envious. We looked good, played well, and proceeded to go undefeated the entire summer. I think I can take some of the credit for making such great uniforms! As insignificant as this experience may seem, it taught me that if I want something, I have to take action toward achieving it. I have often succeeded in implementing my ideas—all it takes is a little courage and some desire to make my ideas a reality.

## Willingness to challenge the status quo

The summer after my first year of college, I found myself painting home exteriors. My brother had gotten into the business and desperately needed painters. Family is very important to me, so I was more than willing to help. Initially, our painting crew included seven members; I was the only girl. When I arrived at job sites, some clients were surprised, even skeptical, to see me standing among the men. By the end of the summer, our crew had dwindled to only three members. The work was tough and physical. I arrived at the job site at 7 a.m. and worked through the day until about 6 or 7 p.m., Monday through Friday, and even some weekends. I did all the work, from scraping and sanding to trimming and roofing.

I impressed many customers with my ability to move 20-foot ladders around the house and scale the roof under the 2 p.m. summer sun. Most people wouldn't expect a girl to do these kinds of jobs. My brother even confessed after the fact that he was uncertain I could handle the strenuous labor, but I surprised him, too. I would never have foreseen doing the work, either, but I learned a lot about commitment and hard work—and I even enjoyed doing it!

## Upbeat personality and social skills

As the daughter of a public speaking coach, communication and confidence in front of crowds have never challenged me. My four years as a varsity cheerleader in high school speak to my energetic and outgoing personality. When I interned in Italy this summer, my boss noticed these traits and commented on how Italians are not as upbeat and enthusiastic as Americans because their economy is worse than the United States'. I couldn't help but laugh when I heard this because he was generalizing about the entire U.S. population based on how I behaved in the office.

The same summer, my dad hosted a dinner party for his colleagues. I helped with preparations and looked forward to meeting some of the people he works with. I initially planned to stay only 15 minutes before heading out of the house for the evening. Those 15 minutes turned into an hour and a half later when I found myself delving into in-depth conversations with these business professionals. Being an outgoing person and a good conversationalist are traits I am very proud to have. Give me five minutes of your time and I will prove it to you as well.

## Self-starter with a desire to help others

During our first year at Notre Dame, some friends and I were discussing how we had had very service-oriented high school experiences but couldn't seem to find our service niche at the University. After some digging around, we discovered that Notre Dame did **not** have a student United Way chapter, despite the closely aligned values of the two institutions. Based on this opportunity, we decided to found a chapter here from scratch.

This process challenged us. It involved many discussions with the Student Activities Office, recruitment of friends and classmates, fundraising efforts, and a search for organizations and people in the South Bend community who needed help. During the lengthy club approval process, we had no money allotted for our club, so we held events such as a dodgeball tournament to finance the service that we had begun to spearhead in the community. The organization we began to work with was an after-school robotics club based out of Riley High School. The club aimed to teach at-risk high school students about technology, while also keeping them out of trouble. A major part of this program was after-school tutoring, which is where we came in. We built strong mentoring relationships with many students and provided them with help in school, as well as in life.

Over the years, my friends and I have slowly begun to pass the torch down to underclassmen in order to make sure the Student United Way at Notre Dame continues to impact the local community positively. Over the past three years, our efforts have directly helped numerous high school students and furthered the relationship between Notre Dame and the local community.

## Tenacity and resilience through defeats

At the beginning of my sophomore year, I noticed something was missing from the dining hall: Quaker Oats' Oatmeal Squares cereal. As an Oatmeal Squares fanatic, I was greatly perturbed. At the end of the previous year, I had made sure friends participated in the survey that would determine the dining hall cereals for the following year. The results had spoken: Oatmeal Squares would return.

Upon discovering at the start of next year they were missing, I immediately contacted the dining hall manager to inquire about the issue. He informed me Quaker Oats had stopped making the cereal. I knew this could not be true, as I had purchased Oatmeal Squares the previous week. I decided to involve myself directly with the issue and personally contacted Quaker Oats. They promptly e-mailed me back, responding that Oatmeal Squares had not been discontinued. They even showed me the closest location where I could purchase them.

I forwarded this information to the dining hall manager, who promised he would look into the problem. A few weeks later, the issue was resolved and Oatmeal Squares returned to the dining hall. Even though it was just cereal, I was determined to take those extra steps to ensure something I loved would live on in the dining hall. The experience increased my confidence in knowing I have the ability to make changes in the world if I apply time and passion to reach my goals.

## Competitiveness and will to succeed

Like many college students, I rely on intermural sports to get my competitive fix because I am no longer a varsity athlete. The women in my dorm, Pasquerilla West (PW), take our team very seriously. As a freshman, despite knowing no one on the team, I was placed on PW's A-team because the captains recognized my desire to succeed and my passion for the sport. The following year, PW went undefeated and ended up winning the championship. This past fall, in my third season, we aimed to come back strong and hoped to earn another chance to win it all. But the second game into the season, I took a wrong turn and ended up tearing my ACL and meniscus and badly spraining every ligament in my knee.

Post-surgery, I could not walk for six weeks. The recovery process moved slowly, but I did everything I could to recover as quickly as possible. Since I could not compete with others, I started to compete with myself. I have pushed myself as hard as I can to get better, to gain a couple more degrees of bending, to lift the extra ten pounds. Challenging myself has offered me a wholly new perspective. Always striving to improve forces me to constantly ask more of myself and try my hardest. It has also encouraged me to support and appreciate others who are on my side, rather as view them as someone to beat.

## Finishing projects and doing so properly and on time

When I saw my college would offer a social media course in the spring semester of my senior year, I knew I had to take that class. At home, my family has completely immersed itself in learning, discussing, and studying the topic, as my dad is the founder of a social media startup. He created a data suite for business intelligence, which monitors customer conversation on social media platforms, analyzes the data, and provides suggestions for companies to improve their social media strategies. Thanks to my dad's startup, I saw firsthand how social media has an impact in the business world. My whole family even analyzed social media responses to Super Bowl ads, poring through thousands of tweets and comments on You Tube videos to determine which ones were the most effective and how companies could use the data to adjust how they delivered to the target audience.

Going into the class, I couldn't wait not just to analyze other companies but also to actually create my own brand and build a social media campaign for it. My team of four classmates created a low-calorie alcohol company, Slender Belle, as a prototype of the brand Skinny Girl, and we presented our recommendations and campaign to top executives at that company at the end of the semester.

During the semester we created a blog and Facebook, Twitter, Hootsuite, YouTube, and Google + accounts for the Slender Belle brand. Consistent themes across all platforms maintained a consistent brand personality and helped us interact with consumers by providing touch points about our products, as well as topics our target customers talk about online. We monitored the hits and interactions posts with consumers and adjusted according to trends we see. For example, we've learned about the importance of the timing of our posts given the lifestyle of our target audience. We've also used the power of Twitter to interact with other strong brands and notable bloggers to increase our reach and following.

Throughout the semester, experts in the social media industry spoke to our class. Their insight increased our awareness of trends in the industry and provided us with new strategies to add to our individual project. Additionally, we closely followed social media bloggers and experts in the field. Social media is a dynamic industry, so we must constantly stay alert for changes.

As a leader of my team, I've encouraged others to try new tactics and think outside the box when interacting with others on social media. Creativity combined with consistency puts social media pages ahead of others and makes them stand out, providing value to consumers.

## Self-discipline and creative problem solving

All senior marketing majors take a course called "Strategic Marketing." Thanks to a recommendation from my former ethics professor, I secured a teaching assistant position a full year and a half before I would take the course myself. Initially, I had a tremendous amount of freedom to develop the structure and plans of the class. Basically, my superiors told me to use the textbook and develop my "dream class." I jumped at the opportunity and capitalized on it to create a class unlike any other at

Notre Dame. Throughout the semester, I reached out to various companies and networked in order to be able to integrate real-life case studies into the class. At the same time, I created the presentations that would be used in class based on the textbook. Again, I considered my general assignment and performed above and beyond by adding my own thoughts and ideas about what topics the Notre Dame marketing classes might not have touched.

Because of my performance, my professor wrote me an unsolicited recommendation letter when it came time to apply for summer internships. This letter helped put my application over the top, and I eventually won the position within Zappos. This year, my professor reached out to me again and asked me to TA for the same class. He said I was the best teaching assistant he had ever had and asked me to join his team for another semester. The TA position reinforced my feeling working with a lot of passion and enthusiasm can elevate any project on which one is working and, in the process, also create lifelong friends and contacts across companies and industries.

## Curiosity and continual development of new skills

At Notre Dame, I work for Fighting Irish Digital Media, the company in charge of all video content for Notre Dame Athletics. I joined the group at the beginning of my sophomore year, and I have thoroughly enjoyed working various sporting events on the weekends. I constantly strive to learn new jobs, from running the camera to working on live event productions. With each new skill I develop, I feel like a better asset to the company with more potential to contribute as much as I can. Although the skills I learn might not directly translate to a future career in marketing, I love this opportunity to learn and develop production skills.

## Experiences in intercultural environments

Last summer, I interned for Silvateam S.p.A., a vegetable extraction company in northern Italy. For a month, I worked on a project with another intern, an Italian. We conducted a survey with Silvateam's clients. My partner would contact Italian clients and I handled international clients. I interacted with people around the world—from Bangladesh to Pakistan to Germany to Brazil. The language barrier, coupled with poor phone connection, often frustrated many of the clients.

I learned a lot about how to bridge international divides and remain calm in challenging situations. Not being able to express myself put me in a very strange place, on top of feeling surrounded by people I perceived as different from myself. In the office, I was the only American. Actually, I was the only American in the entire 2,000-person town, in which English speakers were few and far between. I ate dinner with my boss and various colleagues every weeknight and began to cultivate an appreciation for our conversation. I also started to absorb some of the language. By the end of the summer I could communicate at least brokenly with these colleagues and friends. These interactions helped me to learn more about the Italian culture, to share insights about America, and to appreciate both our similarities and differences.

## Communication skills

Following my involvement with adding recorded music to Notre Dame Stadium, the Athletic Department encouraged me to team with the Leprechaun Legion, the basketball student section spirit group. After attending several meetings, I thought we could leverage the energy and enthusiasm of the group by expanding its reach to all sports, not just basketball. After speaking with the club advisor, I envisioned a re-launch plan and executed it as the newly elected vice president of the Legion. This process involved frequent meetings with the Athletic Department to set up an arrangement that would benefit both the club and department. After holding interviews, I helped select the new board members and we were ready to launch the new face of the Leprechaun Legion in fall 2012.

Along the way, I faced obstacles like pushback from old board members. They saw me as undermining the work they had done, but I reassured them I was simply building off of the foundation they laid. By the end of this year, everyone on the board, both old and new members, have recognized the growth of the group and the great things we accomplished. In just one year, we launched a brand new website and significantly impacted the atmosphere at multiple sporting events.

As a leader, I learned the importance of communication to make people feel included and informed. I also learned how to express my passion in a way that inspires people to buy in to my ideas and to try to match my energy and enthusiasm. Furthermore, I learned that a critical part of being a leader is motivating a group to succeed and to be willing to try new approaches.

## Team player mentality and positive attitude

Last summer, I interned for The Marketing Arm, a sports agency, and immediately put myself in a position of leadership. When I arrived, two project leaders were planning a four-week hospitality program for the Hilton Worldwide owners and developers who would be attending the London 2012 Olympic Games. They communicated with more than 200 guests, so I offered to lead one of the four groups to take some of the pressure off them. Although they had been working on the program for more than a year and I was just starting, they willingly handed over a big part of the project to me. I took charge of all communications and planning for 64 guests. To prepare myself for this role, I studied and immersed myself in the program.

On-site, I faced both emotional and professional challenges. The environment of the hospitality industry was unlike anything I had experienced before. I worked 18 to 20 hour days for four weeks straight without a day off. Some days, exhaustion got the better of my emotions, but I pushed myself to keep going. I supported my team and kept reminding myself of how happy the guests were with the program. That's what made the job so rewarding—we received incredible feedback from guests and teammates. I worked with a smile and learned to troubleshoot issues quickly, staying positive throughout the process and rising as a leader on my team for those who felt down or stressed.

## Detail-oriented

In the fall of my junior year, my marketing research professor tasked groups with selecting a client and helping improve that client's business strategies. My group worked with the Notre Dame business librarians. The two librarians wanted us to research how to improve overall student awareness of the numerous library resources, including a focus on attracting more students to use the library itself. Through our primary and secondary research, which included distributing a survey, we provided a thorough presentation for the librarians at the end of the semester with several suggestions for improvement.

Our research thrilled the librarians, who deeply appreciated the suggestions we presented to two committees. They were even disappointed that all but one of my team members would study abroad the following semester because they wanted to continue working with us. By the time we returned the following fall semester, the library had undergone a broad transformation and had incorporated several of the suggestions we gave them. Three primary ideas implemented:
* Addition of a Café: Au Bon Pain;
* Renovated "fish-bowl" – updating a large open, conversation study room on first floor of the library, by adding things such as new furniture, white boards, new computers etc.;
* 24/7 weekday access for students.

## Desire to take on leadership role

I have been a team player since I was 10 years old. Good leadership is engrained in my brain, and I have participated in numerous development programs. In the yearlong Rosenthal Leadership Academy at Notre Dame, I met with student athletes every Monday to discuss ways we each might be or become great leaders for our athletic teams. While training for this academy, I took a profile test that identified my personality type and leadership style. I scored extremely high as the active type of leader who wants to be well liked, listens to what each team member has to say, and makes the decisions that affect everyone. I pride myself on these qualities and relish any opportunity to take on this roll. I feel that when I lead groups, I have more control over the activities involved, and that with me in the lead, we have a better chance of achieving the goal of our activity.

## Multi-tasking capability

In January 20XX, I was chosen to be a branch manager of a painting company to learn what it takes to be an entrepreneur and run my own business. This was the last commitment I took on for the spring semester on top of two psychology research labs, a job at RecSports, and my participation on the varsity track team. I spread my time very thin as I worked to set up my business, get good grades in all my classes, and have a successful track season. To prepare my business for opening, I had to market and spread awareness, meet with customers to give estimates, book jobs, interview and hire employees, and design a business plan for the summer.

As the semester came to a close, I was ready to open my business. I had undergone some training about how to manage workers and be a good salesman, but I knew little about the actual skill of painting. This ignorance made it challenging to solve production problems and to make executive decisions for my employees. It also caused me to hit a hurdle in the first month of working—my very first EPA job (house containing lead) was probably best described as a nightmare. It was a very old house that needed a lot of work, and I realized on the first day that it was way under-budgeted. Another manager from a neighboring district told me he would not have attempted a job requiring that much prep work, especially one that was about $1,000 under budget. Since the contract price was already signed, there was not much I could do but produce the work. I put my three best painters on the job and decided to work with them to hopefully minimize my losses. My employees were very discouraged so I needed to take extra steps to help them get through the job.

Every day I compiled a strategy for what needed to be accomplished, how long it should take, and who was responsible for it. I encouraged my workers to be as efficient as possible and praised and rewarded them for doing good work. I scheduled my other duties during breaks, lunchtime, and before or after work hours so that I could be on the job site painting as much as my workers were. Even though we still ran over budget, we were able to produce nice work in an efficient manner, and I salvaged a 13% profit margin.

As a leader, I learned from this experience that you should never give up, even when the odds are against you. If you put in enough hard work and make smart, thought-out decisions, you can find a way to succeed. I also learned how to encourage others to meet smaller goals so that as a team we could accomplish the bigger project. Lastly, I gained experience working through negative attitudes in order to accomplish the goal and gain the trust and respect of my employees. I was one of the few managers able to finish out the summer as a successful business owner and, on top of that, I had my highest GPA at Notre Dame.

==============

*How about you? What are some of your leadership stories? Check the list of 'generally desirable attributes' listed above, think back to your experiences meeting challenges in any dimension of your life and start writing. Your leadership stories will help you evidence to would-be employers that you are ready for prime time.*

## Step #2 REVIEW QUESTIONS

1. What background materials will you need to prepare to "sell yourself" to prospective employers?
2. Why is it important to try to bypass the normal large stack of resumes and applications?

3. What are some strategies you can use to try to make the 'Short Stack' right from the get-go?

4. How long will a typical recruiter spend in initially looking at and evaluating your resume?

5. List several important matters to keep in mind when crafting your resume.

6. What is the recommendation for including or excluding your GPA on your resume? How often should you update your resume?

7. True or False: You should never include high school accomplishments on your resume. Why or why not? When/What yes? When/What no?

8. How long should your resume to be when applying for an entry-level position? How about when applying for a more advanced position?

9. What topics should be the focus of your 'leadership stories'?

10. How can you use your Leadership Stories in your job search?

---

1 Primary sources for this section include jeffthecareercoach.com/resume-mistakes/ and monster.com/career-advice/article/how-to-decide-on-resume-length

2 e.g., see 30+ examples of marketing resumes alone at jeffthecareercoach.com/sample-resumes/marketing-resume/; or more than 1000 examples of other resumes at jeffthecareercoach.com/sample-resumes/. You can quickly build a resume using a pre-formatted template of your choice through websites like livecareer.com/builder/rbdesktop/edit-resume.aspx

3 This section synthesizes materials and ideas from themuse.com/advice/how-to-quantify-your-resume-bullets-when-you-dont-work-with-numbers

4 Ibid.

5 This particular example is from jeffthecareercoach.com/resume-mistakes/. So, how did he come up with those numbers? Let's ask:
"How many files per hour do you think you copied using the old process?"
College student: "Probably 15 to 17 per hour"
"Ok, and how many files could you copy with your new process?"
College student: "I'm not sure, but at least 24. I also taught the other employees that were making copies as well"
"Great, how many employees were making copies?"
College student: "Five, counting me."
"Ok. One last question. How much did that job pay per hour?"
College Student: "$10 per hour"
He increased his and the team's productivity from 16 to 24 files per hour, a 50% increase (The number of additional files: 8 divided by his old rate of 16). But that's not all. He saved the company a ton of money. Each person (with benefits, etc.) costs the company $14/hr. On an annual basis, each employee costs $36,000/year. There were five of them, so the cost for all five was $140,000/year. He increased their productivity by 50%. That means he saved the company $70,000/year. Why did he save $70,000? Because now they can do 50% more work which means they could either eliminate half of the positions OR do 50% more files with the same amount of staff.

6 Consider splitting Your GPA. Some students with a low overall cumulative GPA (e.g. 2.8) may have a relatively high GPA in their specialty area (e.g., 3.4). If the specialty area provides a background directly germane for the desired position, split it out. Why not? Being able to achieve at a superior level in any one particular area shows evidence that you can perform at a superior level when focused on a particular area. This may influence some prospective employers; others may be turned off by the mediocre overall performance (2.8 overall GPA) for a variety of reasons you can imagine.

7 monster.com/career-advice/article/how-to-decide-on-resume-length

8 outspokenmedia.com/seo/survey-results-educational-background-of-digital-marketers-seos-revealed/

9 youtube.com/watch?v=inMaGwo-shE

10 Adapted from themuse.com/advice/6-good-reasons-to-always-keep-your-resume-updated

11 See thedailymuse.com/job-search/just-laid-off-your-3-step-action-plan/

12 These initial several paragraphs on what are leadership stories includes some ideas from themuse.com/advice/resume-revamp-how-to-turn-your-duties-into-accomplishments.

# STEP 3

# SEARCHING FOR AN ATTRACTIVE ENTRY-LEVEL POSITION

## QUICK START

You have an abundance of resources available to help you when searching for an entry-level position. Keep an open mind about the process and the variety of job opportunities you encounter.

The search itself will be tedious and frustrating at times but will soon begin paying dividends as you start landing interviews. An array of online and on-campus resources can connect you with opportunities. Your list of potential resources includes, but is not limited to:

- ❖ Your personal and professional networks
- ❖ The Career Center
- ❖ The Career Center job portal
- ❖ University or college job fairs
- ❖ LinkedIn
- ❖ Marketing associations
- ❖ Plethora of job websites: CollegeGrad.com, Glassdoor, Indeed.com, SimplyHired.com, and many more

With so many opportunities available, you must develop a system to filter the job openings. Begin narrowing down categories like the position and type of company that most interest you. You can then proceed to eliminate jobs that don't interest you by applying additional filters from Step 1 such as location, starting salary, etc.

Once you've gathered a set of relevant opportunities, go through another round applying additional filters reviewed in Step 2. These include position descriptions and requirements consistent with your background and interests. Finally, check out each remaining company on Glassdoor for employee views of work-life balance issues and company environment in general. How did employers rate the company? Read some individual reviews. Eliminate companies with generally poor reviews. After this final screening, it's time to start submitting your applications.

# FRAMING YOUR SEARCH

*We start with several important suggestions:*

- ❖  Think positively;
- ❖  Look beyond 'brand-name' companies;
- ❖  Think of your first position as a learning experience.

## Think positively.

When your graduation from college is in view, think of your job search as the first major assignment in your career. Avoid being passive, but don't rush the process. The key is to set aside a little time a few days a week to refine your materials, search for jobs, make connections, and put yourself in a position to succeed.

Companies want to hire good people. Every day, tens of thousands of attractive entry-level positions are begging for solid applicants. With a positive, concerted effort, you will find a match and all your hard work will pay off.

***The bottom line.*** Many companies would love to hire you. They just don't know about you. You have to make that happen!

## Look beyond 'brand-name' companies.

If you insist on your first position being with a "brand-name" company, you may be in for a long and frustrating wait.

Around graduation, it would be great to say proudly to your loved ones that you received an offer and accepted a position with Google, General Mills, Procter & Gamble, General Electric, McKinsey or some other brand-name company. But most attractive entry-level positions are with companies you have likely never heard of. Who can name:

- ❖  600 marketing and advertising agencies in Chicago alone?[1]
- ❖  Or 3,000+ advertising jobs available at any one time in NYC?[2]
- ❖  Or 1,500+ in Los Angeles?[3]

It is very likely that you will not have even heard of 90 percent or more of the prospective employers included in the thousands of entry-level marketing jobs listed by on line job search services (reviewed below). But that is where most of the jobs are.

***The bottom line.*** You do not have to work for a company that everyone knows. There are ten times more entry-level positions with unfamiliar than with familiar brand-name companies. After you get some experience, you will have plenty of time and opportunities to move to other companies, including brand-name companies, if that is still important to you.

# Think of your first position as a learning experience.

Just like graduating college, landing a job is simply one checkpoint in your career—it's not the finish line. You aren't making a commitment to work for your first company or in your first position for the rest of your life. Pick an acceptable position and start. Your career will take many turns before it's over, but it all starts with the first offer. [4] In sum, your first company and position will not be your last.

By the time you are 30, you and all of your friends will have changed your companies and positions three, four, five times ***or more.*** Look at some random profiles of your LinkedIn contacts for convincing evidence. The two examples below provide the marketing employment history of two representative young professionals who recently spoke to a class at Notre Dame. ***Nearly all of our speakers (former students, generally) changed positions and changed companies numerous times.***

Your first position does not commit you to a specific career. You will worry less and maintain a much more positive outlook if you think of your first job as an opportunity to:

  ❖ Get important experience to strengthen your resume and leadership stories;
  ❖ Build your professional network—your next position will in all likelihood come from someone in that network;
  ❖ Discover which parts of the day-to-day work you like and dislike in terms of:
    ❖ What you specifically want to do each day;
    ❖ What products and/or services you do and do not like to work with;
    ❖ Where (geographically) you want to work;
    ❖ What daily work schedule you prefer;
    ❖ Who determines what you do and when you work;
    ❖ How effectively you can work independently, when setting your own schedule—e.g., working from home on occasion;
    ❖ What compensation and benefits you need, including time-off policies such as annual vacation days, holidays, sick leave, flex time;
    ❖ How much you do or do not working as part of a team:
    ❖ What kind of relationship you enjoy or do not enjoy with your immediate superior;
    ❖ What kind of colleague relationships you prefer.

***The bottom line.*** Your first position will not be perfect. It is the first of many steps in your marketing career, and it does not lock in a career or even a career direction.

## Example 1

Four companies, four positions in four years—not unusual.

1. **Digital Marketing Associate**
   SIM Partners - July 2013 – Present (1 year 8 months) Greater Chicago Area
2. **Account Executive Humana**
   Humana - May 2012 – July 2013 (1 year 3 months) Madison, Wisconsin Area
3. **Public Relations Director**
   The Green Observer - August 2011 – May 2012 (10 months) Champaign, IL
4. **Office Assistant**
   University of Illinois College of Business - August 2010 – May 2012 (1 year 10 months)

## Example 2

Five companies, eleven positions in fourteen years—not at all unusual.

1. **Director, Digital Communications and Creative Services**
   Alcoa - September 2014 – Present (6 months) Pittsburgh, PA
2. **Director of Social Media**
   General Nutrition Centers, Inc - August 2013 – Present (1 year 7 months) Pittsburgh, PA
3. **Co-owner**
   Tender Bar + Kitchen - March 2013 – Present (2 years)
4. **Co-owner**
   Verde Mexican Kitchen & Cantina - 2011 – Present (4 years) Greater Pittsburgh Area
5. **Sr. Manager, Digital Marketing**
   HJ Heinz - February 2012 – July 2013 (1 year 6 months) Greater Pittsburgh Area
6. **Brand Manager - Foodservice Ketchup**
   HJ Heinz - March 2011 – February 2012 (1 year) Pittsburgh, PA
7. **Associate Brand Manager - Foodservice Ketchup**
   HJ Heinz - August 2008 – February 2011 (2 years 7 months) Pittsburgh, PA
8. **Brand Management Intern - Foodservice**
   HJ Heinz - 2007 – 2007 (less than a year)
9. **Premier Account Manager**
   Verizon Business - June 2004 – June 2006 (2 years 1 month)
10. **Global Client Services Manager**
    Verizon Business/MCI/UUNet - December 2000 – May 2004 (3 years 6 months)
11. **Global Client Services Representative**
    Verizon Business/MCI/UUNet - June 2000 – November 2000 (6 months)

# EXECUTING THE SEARCH

Once you have an idea of the type of entry-level marketing position (or positions) you would like to pursue (Step 1) and after you have developed and refined your resume and leadership stories (Step 2), your next set of challenges involves:

❖ Finding opportunities; then

- ❖ Filtering & evaluating opportunities; then
- ❖ Selecting opportunities to pursue.

# Find opportunities.

Finding available entry-level marketing positions is not difficult today, given the proliferation of job search websites and companies. These sites identify thousands of available positions—positions begging for attractive candidates.

For example, at the time of writing:

- ❖ Indeed.com lists 24,578 full-time entry-level marketing jobs, about 10,000 of which offer annual salaries of more than $45,000.[5] The site lists nearly 2,000 in NYC[6] and 1,000 each in Chicago and Los Angeles.
- ❖ LinkedIn lists more than 34,000 entry-level marketing jobs, of which more than half offer full-time work with annual salaries of more than $40,000.[7]
- ❖ Simply Hired lists 150 entry-level positions in advertising alone in Chicago.[8]

Below we review some of the many job sites and offer tips for using a few of the more important and popular ones to uncover available entry-level marketing positions. Knowing where to start looking can be overwhelming, especially with online job search services. The following is a list of some of the best and most useful job search tools and sites to help launch your marketing career.

## The career center

The place to start your job search is closest to home. Most universities and colleges have a career center to help students find jobs and summer internships. Unfortunately, many students are not aware of and/or do not utilize the wide range of resources the college career centers provide. From professional contacts, to resume, cover letter and follow-up tips, to mock interviews, to perspectives on proper dress and etiquette, these centers offer a broad array of valuable services just for you! The professionals working at your career center want to help you with your job search. It is their job and their passion to do just that. Take advantage of it!

## Career center job portal

Most career centers also provide an online job search resource. This is typically a database containing an assortment of full-time and internship positions and is strictly for students attending that particular college or university. The job opportunities listed come from the hundreds of employers that have relations with the particular university or college. This is significant because the companies posting on this website are specifically seeking out students from your school. This gives you a leg up on candidates from other schools for available positions at these particular companies. Take advantage of it!

## University or college job fairs

Most career centers hold on campus job fairs a couple of times each academic year. These fairs offer great job search opportunities. For one, like the job portal sites, companies attending your school's job fairs are interested in hiring students specifically from your school. Second, job fairs generally have a relaxed environment that makes it easy to introduce yourself to business professionals and begin building your network of contacts. Finally, in a very short period of a couple hours, a career fair provides you with the opportunity to introducing yourself to recruiters from multiple different companies of interest. Elsewhere (see Step 5 - Interview Strategies and Tips) we provide some important tips on how to prepare for and how to approach recruiters from different target companies at career fairs. With proper preparation and using a practiced, professional manner, career fairs provide an outstanding opportunity to move you on to the second interview stage for specifically targeted companies and positions.

## LinkedIn

LinkedIn is more than a social networking site. It includes an immense, unique database full of job opportunities just waiting to be explored. An entire section on the website is nested under the "Jobs" tab, in which you can apply different filters depending upon your job preferences. Even better, as soon as you find a company with an open position, you can then research current employees at that same company.[9] This unique feature of LinkedIn can help you to get a better understanding of multiple potentially relevant positions at the company as well as to key people who could be potential sponsors for you. We provide more expansive coverage of LinkedIn, including examples, later in this step.

## Marketing Associations

Many marketing organizations provide job boards on which they post regularly post new opportunities. For example, the American Marketing Association maintains a job board that includes positions all over the country, not just in major cities—a unique asset if you're looking to get into a specific field in a specific location. The site allows you to separate internships from full time opportunities and to filter your search by specialties and industry as well. Other marketing organizations that offer robust job portals are the Public Relations Society of America (PRSA) and the Direct Marketing Association (DMA). Check these out.

## Collegegrad.com

Collegegrad.com caters to recent graduates by gathering entry-level positions, including both internships and full-time opportunities. An Advanced filtering system enables you to browse and filter available positions by job level, title, industry, location, and employer, and other options to narrow your range of alternative jobs to explore. The site links these positions to Glassdoor (covered next), where you can read a more in-depth description and further information on the relevant company (e.g., other employees' experiences at the company, CEO rankings, etc.).

## Glassdoor

Glassdoor is much more than a job search site. The website provides professionals with company reviews and ratings, information on salaries, and interview questions to expect for specific companies and positions. The actual job search portal on the website has the unique "Company Ratings" filter. Glassdoor rates each company on a scale from one to four stars, which helps give applicants an idea of the company culture, work-life balance, and more. We provide more expansive coverage of Glassdoor, including examples, later in Step 3 and again in later steps.

## Indeed.com

Indeed.com is an overall job search portal rather than one strictly for marketing, but it is still a very useful website to consider when looking for entry-level marketing positions. The site begins by asking for the specific job title, keywords, or company you're looking at, combined with the city or state of interest. You can filter positions by salary estimate, location and many other variable as well. We present an example of using Indeed.com later in Step 3.

## SimplyHired.com

SimplyHired.com is similar to Indeed in that the base criteria asks for the job title, company, and city or state of interest. It also includes the option to input your unique skills for further filtering. The site's advanced search goes into more specifics—under the "special filters" section of the website, you can frame your search with unique categories such as "Veteran Friendly," "LGBT Friendly," "New Graduate," or "Fortune 500." Simply Hired is generally regarded as a particularly good job search site if for those who have not narrowed down what jobs might be of primary interest.[10] We include an example of using Simplyhired.com later in Step 3.

----

Job and career agencies such as Indeed.com, Simple Hired, College Grad.com as well as others such as Career Rookie, Monster.com and many, many others want to hear from you because they make their money by matching qualified candidates like you with companies looking for you. Use these resources.

-----

The resources and websites reviewed above are but a handful of the many services available for career and job searching. For example, your personal and professional networks and Google provide additional valuable job search resources to pursue.

* ❖ *Your personal and professional networks.* Consider acquaintances from home, from your internship(s), from your relatives, from friends who graduated a year or two ago, from friends back home, and others. Do not overlook these—you need to start somewhere, so why not take advantage of your existing contacts? We expand upon these.

❖ ***Google.*** Search for the entry-level position(s) you think you want (and feel qualified for) and the city where you would like to work. You will find multiple employment services, including those mentioned above as well as others like Career Rookie and Monster.

# Filter and evaluate opportunities.

Your next challenge is to narrow down your list of potential entry-level marketing opportunities to a smaller set of positions that closely match your interests and qualifications. You can begin this process by using filters built into most of the job search engines reviewed above—to quickly screen for more attractive personal options.

## Apply your first filters.

Your first filters to apply are those you picked in Step 1, including your desired type of entry-level position, your desired type of company, and your other limiting factors. These initial questions enable you to narrow down and focus your search. To review:

### Which marketing positions are of greatest interest to you?

❖ Sales and sales management—consumer or business-to-business products and services
❖ Retail—analysis and planning at corporate level or in-store retail sales, merchandising, or store management
❖ Public relations
❖ Market data analytics and market research
❖ Digital, interactive, and social media marketing
❖ Brand and product management
❖ Advertising and promotion (e.g., strategy, media planning, creative and design)
❖ For others, refer back to the specific examples reviewed in Step 1

### What type of companies most interests you?

❖ What, if any, particular industry interests you?
❖ What, if any, particular location do you prefer?
❖ What companies offer your ideal culture and work-life balance?
❖ What, if any, particular size company most interests you? Would you prefer to work for small or medium-sized business or a large corporation?
❖ Would you work for a not-for-profit entity?

### Do you have other potential limiting factors?

❖ Are you looking only for full-time positions?
❖ Is an internship with the prospect of a full time offer at end acceptable?
❖ Is a rotational training program required?

❖   What is the minimum salary you will accept?
❖   Ideally, how many hours would you work in an average week?
❖   How many weeks of paid time off do you want?
❖   What is your minimum for signing bonus and/or moving expenses?
❖   Do you have other limitations or preferences?

*Start your filtering process with these limiting factors. We will next explain and give examples of this process.*

## Example

Assume that our ideal entry-level job would be in advertising in Chicago. Start by Googling "Entry level advertising jobs in Chicago." A number of the most popular job search sites immediately pop up. Next, let's evaluate the results from some of these sites, including Indeed, Simply Hired, Glassdoor, and LinkedIn.

 **entry level advertising jobs in chicago**

**Entry Level Advertising Jobs, Employment in Chicago, IL | Indeed.com**
www.indeed.com/q-Entry-Level-Advertising-l-Chicago,-IL-jobs.html ▾ Indeed.com ▾
Jobs 1 - 10 of 168 - 168 Entry Level Advertising Jobs available in Chicago, IL on Indeed.com. one
search. all jobs.
You've visited this page 2 times. Last visit: 4/9/16

**2016 Advertising Entry-level Jobs in Chicago, IL**
https://www.looksharp.com/s/advertising-entry-level-jobs/chicago-il ▾
Find a 2016 advertising Entry-level Job in Chicago, IL. There's no better time than right now to take on
advertising entry-level jobs. These starting advertising ...

**Full Time Entry Level Marketing Advertising Jobs in Chicago, IL ...**
www.monster.com/jobs/q-full-time-entry-level-marketing-advertising-jo... ▾ Monster.com ▾
Currently, there are no Full Time Entry Level Marketing Advertising jobs available in Chicago, Illinois
which match this search. You may wish to explore similar ...

**Advertising Jobs in Chicago, IL | LinkedIn**
www.linkedin.com › Jobs › Advertising Jobs ▾ LinkedIn ▾
Apply to 3095 Advertising jobs in Chicago, IL on LinkedIn. ... so we are now looking for the next
generation of entry level candidates to train in customer service .

**Junior Marketing Associates Entry Level Advertising Jobs in Chicago, IL**
www.careerbuilder.com/jobs-junior-marketing-associates-entry-level-ad... ▾ CareerBuilder ▾
Entry Level Sales & Management CM is looking to fill positions in their marketing, sales & PR
department. CM is a privately owned and operated advertising, ...

**Entry Level Marketing / Entry Level Management / Entry Level ...**
www.careerbuilder.com/jobseeker/jobs/jobdetails.aspx?job_did... ▾ CareerBuilder ▾
Premier Chicago, IL 5/8/2016 ... Premier is looking for both entry level and experienced marketing
representatives to grow with our firm. ... marketing, student, accounting, entrepreneur, summer job, entry
level, sales, marketing, general, retail, ... business, internship, advertising, human resources, entry level,
retail, insurance, ...

**Entry Level Advertising Jobs | Glassdoor**
https://www.glassdoor.com/Job/entry-level-advertising-jobs-SRCH_KO0,23.... ▾ Glassdoor ▾
Search Entry Level Advertising jobs. Get the right Entry Level Advertising job with company ratings
& salaries. 6389 open jobs for Entry Level Advertising.

**Advertising Jobs in Chicago, IL | Simply Hired**
www.simplyhired.com/search?q=advertising&l=chicago,+il ▾
Job Window Enterprises - Chicago, IL. Attention all Marketing & Advertising Grads! We have entry
level openings that meet your experience requirements ...

Consider Indeed.com At the time of writing, the search for "Entry Level Advertising jobs in Chicago" reveals 191 potential job opportunities, as shown in the exhibit.

Note the filters on the left. To reduce the 191 results to a more manageable number, let's apply some limiting factors, such as "full time" (177 available) and salary of "$45,000+" (69 available). Applying both criteria yields 62 jobs available, with 42 in downtown Chicago if you want to add that criterion as well.

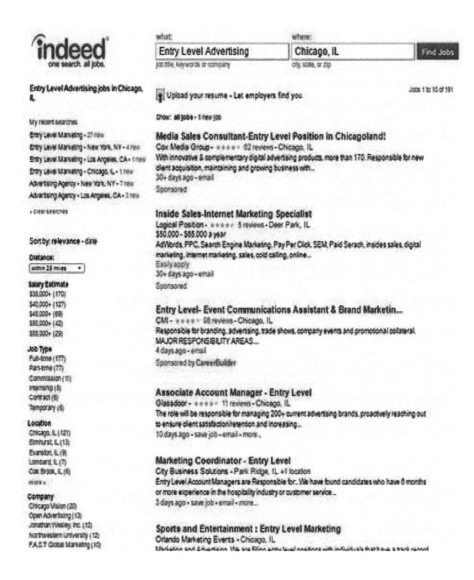

Next, SimplyHired shows 145 entry-level advertising jobs available near Chicago.

### SimplyHired

| Entry Level Advertising | Chicago, IL |
|---|---|

**Showing 1-50 of 145 Entry Level Advertising jobs near Chicago, IL**

**Refine your search** Clear Filters

| Sort by | Date Added | Distance | More Filters | | Show |
|---|---|---|---|---|---|
| Relevance ▼ | Anytime ▼ | 25 miles ▼ | None Selected ▼ | | 50 Jobs ▼ |

**Public Relations and Communications Assistant - Entry Level** SimplyApply
Premier - Chicago, IL
Public Relations and Communications Assistant - Entry Level The Job Window has an immediate need for a Public Relations and Marketing Communications Assistant to join ...
23 days ago, Sponsored by The Job Window

**Entry Level Retail Sales Agent**
Career Hub - Naperville, IL
CUSTOMER SERVICE EXPERIENCE WANTED! Entry Level Retail Sales Agent? Openings! If you have great people skills and enjoy working with the public, we want to meet ...
4 hours ago, Sponsored by Career Hub

**Entry Level Marketing, Advertising & Sales Assistant**
Mac Collective - Elmhurst, IL
Job Description: Entry Level Marketing, Advertising & Sales Assistant All entry level applicant are welcome apply, we provide full product training to all entry level applicants ...
1 day ago, Sponsored by ZipRecruiter

**Entry Level Marketing / Advertising / PR - NO Experience Necessary!**
Zengo&co - Chicago, IL
Job Description: Zengo&Co is seeking a driven, action oriented individual to join our sales team as a Business Development Representative. In this entry level role as a ...
3 days ago, Sponsored by ZipRecruiter

**COLLEGE GRADS & INTERNS- Entry Level Marketing & Advertising**
OTF - Chicago, IL
Job Description: COLLEGE GRADS & INTERNS- Entry Level Marketing & Advertising Positions INTERNSHIPS, FULL TIME AND PART TIME ENTRY LEVEL POSITIONS ...
1 day ago, Sponsored by ZipRecruiter

Under "More Filters" (toward top center), one can click on the filters to reduce the 145 to a more manageable number for closer evaluation. Let's apply some limiting factors, such as 'full time' (under 'job type') (142 available) and 'new graduate' (under special filters) (114 available). Applying both criteria still yields 72 jobs available. The filter shows 61 of these are available in downtown Chicago if you would want to add that criteria as well (within five miles of Chicago instead of 25).

Next, try Glassdoor, showing 436 entry-level advertising jobs available in Chicago.

As stated earlier, Glassdoor's unique filters are not only easy to use, but they also include company ratings from current employees. These ratings come from current and former employees' answers to questions like, "Would you recommend this company to a friend?" You can also access specific comments of employees who provided the evaluations. We will further discuss on Glassdoor ratings later.

Let's apply some limiting factors, such as "entry level" (under "job type"—339 of the 436 available jobs) and "full time" (also under job type—251 available). It is not possible to apply both criteria simultaneously on Glassdoor. The filter shows 193 entry-level jobs are available in downtown Chicago, if you want to add that as well—set your search to within five miles of Chicago instead of 25 miles.

Let's say of the 193 downtown entry-level advertising jobs, you would only want to work for a company with an employee rating of at least 3.0 (out of 5.0). Applying this filter yields 131 remaining positions.

Finally, let's try LinkedIn, which offers strong, but much more inclusive, filters (perhaps too inclusive for some new graduates). At the time of writing, 667 entry-level advertising jobs in Chicago appear on LinkedIn.

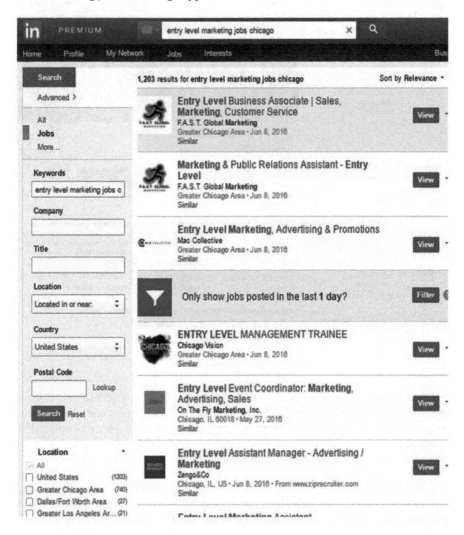

LinkedIn's filters appear on the left. To reduce the 667 to a more manageable number, let's apply some limiting factors, such as your "experience level." "Entry level" now yields 312 available jobs, while limiting to salary to "$40,000+" results in 115. Applying both criteria yields 62 jobs. The filter shows 55 of these are in downtown Chicago, if you limit that criterion as well.

### Continue your filtering.

So far, using the various search engines and their filters, you would have narrowed down the available "entry-level advertising jobs in Chicago" from many hundreds to somewhere between 42 and 131 potential opportunities. Using any single engine, you could narrow them down further, but let's stop using the built-in filters at this point, for fear of screening out too many opportunities without a closer look.

Next, scan the job titles and company names for each opportunity left in the search engines. Some jobs will appear in more than one engine, but don't worry about that. Scan all the engines you used, lest you overlook some prime opportunities.

You will likely instantly dismiss many opportunities because the job title or name of the company do not fit the criteria you set in Step 1 for **marketing positions of greatest interest to you and the type of company that most interests you.** So be it. You should easily be left with 20 to 30 or perhaps more opportunities that appear to be consistent with your initial preferences from Step 1.

## Apply your second filters.

Your second filters help you identify opportunities with descriptions and requirements that match your capabilities and record. For the 20 to 30+ remaining search results, read each job description and list of requirements. Ask yourself:

- ❖ Does that sound like me?
- ❖ Would I enjoy doing that?
- ❖ Am I qualified to do that?
- ❖ Do the needs of that job match my strengths?
- ❖ When interviewing, could my stories (from Step 2) prove that I do indeed have the interest, relevant experience, knowledge, and capabilities required?

## Example

Digital Marketing Paid Media Account Manager (for Spectrum Communications—Chicago)

### *Description*
"Are you data-savvy? Do you love analyzing trends and picking out the most important parts? As a Digital Marketing Paid Media Account Manager for Spectrum, you will work alongside other enthusiastic and knowledgeable analytical and data-driven professionals to aid in creating, setting up, and executing Internet marketing plans. We develop customized solutions for our clients that consistently generate quality leads via digital marketing on sources such as AdWords, Bing, and Facebook. You will also be organizing, managing, and analyzing large data sets and drawing out relevant insights. If you're a lover of all things numbers or data, this could be the perfect position for you!"

### *Responsibilities*
As a Digital Marketing Paid Media Account Manager, you will support the goals and objectives of our clients by:

- ❖ Planning and executing paid search campaigns, including, but not limited to, account setup, strategy development, organization, management, attending client meeting, and reporting.

* Providing regular reporting and analysis to clients and account managers.
* Analyzing keyword data and identifying negative keywords.
* Evaluating large pools of data; identifying trends and applying new insights to client campaigns.
* Managing return on investments related to advertising budgets.
* Staying up-to-date on the latest trends in search marketing

### Requirements

We are as passionate about great technology as we are passionate about working with great people. At Spectrum we are seeking someone who shares these passions. We also would like you to have:

* A bachelor's degree in marketing, business, or a related field
* At least 2 years of professional SEO/SEM experience
* Account/client management experience
* PPC management experience
* A fundamental understanding of how websites are built
* A fundamental understanding of HTML and CSS
* An active understanding of the search marketing industry
* Ability to understand and develop performance reports using Google Analytics Data
* Exceptional communication skills, both verbal and written
* Project management experience (a plus)

Now ask yourself, *"Does that sound like me?"* Would I enjoy doing that? Am I qualified? Do the needs of that job match my strengths? Do I have good stories to prove I have the requisite interests, experience, and general knowledge required?

* If no, dismiss this opportunity.
* If yes, or "pretty sure I do," leave it in your mix.

Move on down the list of your remaining 20 to 30+ opportunities. You will likely see an array of "job requirements" like any of those in the example—we have included more examples in an Appendix to this Chapter. For each alternative, ask the same questions: "Do my interests and proven qualifications fit this opportunity?" Reject off-hand those of little interest and those for which your background and proven qualifications fall well short of the requirements.

## Don't necessarily let "experience requirements" stop you.

Don't be too hard in self-evaluating your relevant qualifications—it is unlikely that any candidate will meet and clearly prove they possess all of these requirements in spades. This is particularly true regarding the "experience requirement" that appears in many job requirement lists, even for entry-level jobs.

For example, a brand new college graduate landed the above "Digital Account Manager" position without strictly meeting the formal requirement of "at least 2 years of professional SEO/SEM experience." Any formal and informal experiences you have had during college count! For example, while this young person had no formal experience with SEO/SEM (much less, "2 years"), she did study it as one topic in a Social Media course. From that experience and from reading more about it and viewing some SEO/SEM videos prior to her interview, she readily received (& accepted) the offer.

# Refine your materials to better match the key requirements of a targeted position.

Let's say that one of the 20+ relevant jobs you have uncovered with the search engines strongly appeals to you, and you feel you could be a pretty good fit. When you originally developed your resume and stories, however, you may not have been aware that such opportunities even existed. As a result, your resume and stories do not match well with the stated requirements of this attractive position.

## What to do?

* ❖ Rework your resume.
* ❖ Assuming you have experiences that match the most vital requirements, list them, expand them, and place them prominently on your resume.
* ❖ Rework and/or retitle some of your stories to create a better match.
* ❖ Develop new stories to fill some obvious gaps.

## Get qualified: fill gaps in your background and resume.

If you get your heart set on a specific job type for which you do not have credentials for serious consideration, it is never too late to become qualified!

* ❖ Start reading and studying and perhaps take an online course to fill any particularly important requirements for that position that you do not have.
* ❖ **Appendix 2** to this chapter presents an example of how someone not currently qualified in digital marketing might upgrade her or his knowledge, experience, and, most importantly, visibility.
* ❖ The principles demonstrated in that appendix apply to job areas of marketing that you find very attractive, but for which you do not currently feel adequately qualified. For entry-level positions especially, employers' expectations for background and experience are not sky-high.

# One more screen: Glassdoor

Glassdoor boasts a large database of company reviews and promotes itself as giving job seekers insights into a company's work conditions, interview processes, salaries, and benefits. In addition to providing job listings, Glassdoor allows employers to identify job candidates and market their companies to job seekers. [11]

We strongly suggest that you use Glassdoor as your final screening device before you start applying for any positions (covered in the next Step). Glassdoor tells you what current employees think about their company. Would they recommend it to a friend?

Do you approve of the CEO? Answers to those questions can provide valuable perspectives. Consider a few examples.

Let's look at the reviews of Google on Glassdoor.

No wonder so many recent grads want to work at Google. Of the 4,000+ employee reviews, 91 percent would recommend working at Google to a friend, 98 percent approve of the CEO, and the company gets an impressive overall rating of 4.4.

Now, let's check Amazon.

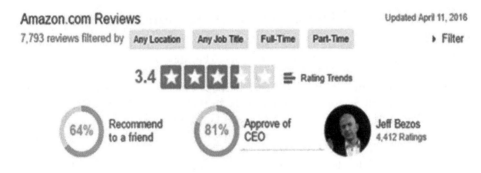

Glassdoor's Amazon ratings are relatively weak. Of 7,000+ employee reviews, 64 percent would recommend the company to a friend, 81% approve of the CEO, and the company gets an overall rating of only 3.4. None are comparatively good ratings.

But what if Amazon approached you, having accessed your resume and credentials on one the websites we have recommended above. What then, when you spy these relatively low ratings? *We would not suggest using the low ratings to automatically dismiss any company or opportunity.* Rather, you should now carefully explore a subset of the good and bad reviews, then use the same discerning eye for the interviews.

Glassdoor's rich filters enable you to get the reviews and interviews for specific positions, i.e., the position for which you are considering applying. Look at more recent ratings versus older ones—perhaps things are getting better for employees, perhaps much better, or perhaps not. So, cruise around the Glassdoor site for Amazon, learn what makes the company tick, learn what some folks are obviously upset about. Those employee perspectives can suggest some good questions for you to ask if you ultimately apply and advance to the interview stage.

Next, let's check a mid-size ERP Software company, NetSuite. NetSuite has about 3,000 employees and 437 reviews, so it is safe to assume this is a reasonable sample.

NetSuite's ratings are not as high as Google's, but they are solid—82 percent of employees would recommend it to a friend, 93 percent approve of the CEO, and the company gets an overall rating of 4.0. Those ratings certainly warrant keeping NetSuite in your mix, if it is one of the companies you are considering.

Finally, let's check a smaller software company of 120 to 150 employees, with 22 Glassdoor reviews and 27 interviews.

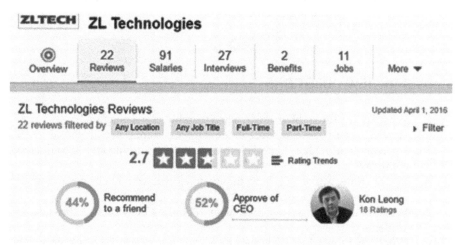

ZL's ratings are a red flag if that company is in your mix. Only 44 percent would recommend it to a friend, only 52 percent approve of the CEO, and the company gets an overall rating of only 2.7. What if you received an offer out of the blue from this company? These ratings might suggest an automatic reject, but why not look more closely? If you did, you would see a significant uptrend in most recent ratings, which warrant a close look at each review, as well as the interviews and other data and information on Glassdoor for ZL.

We suggest the following general principles when viewing Glassdoor ratings to provide perspectives for your screening.

❖ Use Glassdoor as a later filter. Explore Glassdoor information only after you have applied your filters from Step 1 (your desired position and company type) and your filters from Step 2 (identifying opportunities with descriptions and requirements that match your capabilities and record).

❖ Pay attention to sample size. If only a handful of employees have provided ratings (regardless of company size), do not put too much stock in the Glassdoor ratings. At the same time, as long as you have looked it up, do read the reviews and interview tips, as they may be helpful as you continue to pursue this particular opportunity (Step 3).

❖ Pay attention to more recent ratings. Put more credence and weight on these. This is especially true if everything else about a particular opportunity and company seems to align with your preferences and qualifications.

❖ Finally, roam all around any relevant company's Glassdoor page. Most Glassdoor company pages include a wealth of information not available from other job search engines. This is due to the breadth of coverage and the fact that input comes from employees, not the company itself or from third party sources. Just for your information, check out Glassdoor for a few well-known companies, then cruise around and see the wealth of insightful information available for any would-be new employees.

## Step #3 REVIEW QUESTIONS

1. What are the three things to do when searching for a position?
2. How many entry-level jobs are looking for applicants every day?
3. Upon graduation, how likely is it that you will be working for a 'brand name' company?
4. By the time you're 30, how many times will you likely have changed companies and/or positions?
5. What kinds of resources does your school's Career Center provide for students?
6. What other tools does Glassdoor have aside from the job search component of the website?

7.  Name three filters that can be applied to your job search when searching sites such as Glassdoor, Indeed.com, Simply.Hired.com, LinkedIn, or others?
8.  What question should you ask yourself when looking at job descriptions?
9.  Give an example of how you can get around 'Experience Requirements.'
10. If a company that has low ratings on Glassdoor approaches you, should you automatically dismiss them because of these ratings? If not, what should you do?

# Appendix 1: Examples of Job Requirements for a number of different marketing positions.

### Starcom Media Associate – Job Requirements
❖ Quantitative and analytical skills
❖ Top-notch communication skills (verbal and written)
❖ Experience developing and presenting your thoughts and ideas
❖ Critical thinking, willing to analyze everything and look for unconventional solutions to problems
❖ Willingness to speak up with new ideas and challenge the status quo
❖ Help carry out the smart ideas of others
❖ Detail oriented
❖ Exceptional organizational skills
❖ Thrive on a team
❖ Can meet tight deadlines
❖ Comfortable juggling multiple priorities
❖ Enjoy managing projects and/or processes and can talk about experiences in this area
❖ Enjoy learning and are willing to lean in to new opportunities
❖ Embrace a role that requires a mix of art and science
❖ Highly proficient in Microsoft Excel, PowerPoint and Word as well as other equivalent programs

### Leo Burnett Strategist – Job Requirements
❖ Deep curiosity about human behavior
❖ Open to diversity of thought, culture, people, etc.
❖ Appreciation for the arts and creativity; actively seeks out creative content
❖ Curious about marketing, media, business, new communication platforms
❖ Ability to tolerate, embrace, even thrive on ambiguity
❖ Highly collaborative approach to sparking, building, and sharing ideas; must have strong ability to collaborate within department, agency, and, when applicable, on multi-agency teams
❖ Exceptional communication skills; ability to tell a compelling story and synthesize info
❖ Data interpretation and analytic skills; familiarity with research methodologies
❖ Resiliency and analytic skills; familiarity with research

- Integrated campaign experience, including experience with digital/social media
- Strong foundation in qualitative and quantitative research fundamentals
- Demonstrate strong conceptual thinking skills
- Combine analytical rigor with creative problem-solving skills
- Display personal initiative and ownership of work

Strong teamwork and interpersonal skills

## Jack Morton Associate Strategist

- Confidence
- Risk-taking
- Ability to collect, read, analyze, interpret and synthesize information from a variety of sources and develop strategic insights and points of view
- Strong verbal and written communication skills, including engaging presentation skills
- Motivated
- Exceptional concepting and writing skills
- Proficiency in branding, social, and experiential marketing concepts
- Ability to create concepts and copy that deliver on project briefs and align to business goals
- Ability to create concepts and copy that deliver
- Strong command of the English language with an eye for grammatical errors and a background in multiple style guides
- Ability to work in a fast-paced, high-pressure environment

## Energy BBDO Community Manager

- Strong understanding of how to take on a brand voice, how people interact with brands in social, and how to quell potential issues
- Stay ahead of social trends to assist in ongoing education for internal teams
- Exemplary verbal and written communication skills
- Evaluate past creative performance to inform future creative development
- Digital photography skills and an eye for visual content
- Knowledge of digital monitoring and reporting processes and tools
- Excels at research, possesses excellent writing skills
- Proficiency in Microsoft Office products
- Dedicated to blogging, micro blogging and use of Facebook
- Demonstrated creativity and documented immersion in social media
- Demonstrated ability to map out a marketing strategy and drive it by testing and metrics
- Experience sourcing and managing content development and publishing
- Ability to jump from the creative side of marketing to the analytical side, able to demonstrate why their ideas are analytically sound
- Ability to work with multiple teams simultaneously
- Knowledge of search engine optimization basics including basic keyword research
- Proven organizational skills and ability to handle multiple projects while meeting deadlines

❖ Ability to communicate results to management and in a fast paced environment

## Appendix 2: An example of getting qualified: filling gaps in your background and resume

Let's say the digital marketing opportunity above appeals to you, but your package would not likely get you even to the short stack, much less through the interview process. What might you do to upgrade your digital skills and presence?

Most folks working in digital today (2016) had little if any formal education in digital marketing. They learned it on their own. How can you learn about and then evidence your passion and experience in digital? You might try strategies such as these to beef up your visibility, resume, and stories to better match requirement of digital marketing positions.

❖ Grow your social media accounts.
❖ Start and boost an Instagram account: document how it grew and how you achieved it.
❖ Promote photos of your favorite places.
❖ Document how you built up your followers.
❖ Start a Reddit account, grow it, document the growth, and indicate how you did it.
❖ Start a blog—this is an awesome way to stand out from others.
❖ Blog about your personal-professional learning and development over time (e.g., your marketing skills, digital stuff you question, and/or answers you found or are still looking for
❖ Interviewers can only find out so much about you in a 15-minute interview— refer them to or show them your blog that talks about your personal and professional growth with your areas of marketing interest (e.g., digital analytics, design, research, media planning, etc.)
❖ On your blog, always be asking questions about things you are trying to learn. Question new strategies, campaigns, theories you are reading about.
❖ Keep a log documenting your learning as you watch videos and review case studies.
❖ Launch a mini-web-site, or build a free Wordpress.com site.
❖ Just having a page up and trying to improve its rank would put you way ahead of the crowd.
❖ Pick a keyword that is not very competitive and get it ranked—spend a couple hours per month reading about and trying different strategies to
❖ Benchmark its starting rank, then test different strategies to optimize it.
❖ Document how you moved from rank from "X" to "Y."

Now you have some impressive new "Digital lines' to place at the top of your resume and great new digital stories to talk about in your interviews for that digital position.

---

3 indeed.com/jobs?q=Advertising+Agency&l=Los+Angeles%2C+CA

4 Insights and content in this paragraph are from inc.com/samuel-edwards/great-job-sites-for-recent-college-graduates.html

5 indeed.com/q-Entry-Level-Marketing-jobs.html

6 indeed.com/jobs?q=Entry+Level+Marketing&l=New+York%2C+NY&rs=1

7 linkedin.com/jobs/entry-level-marketing-jobs

8 simplyhired.com/search?q=advertising+intern&l=chicago%2C+il See more on this and other employment agencies below.

9 marketing.about.com/od/exploremarketingcareers/a/Where-To-Find-And-Post-Marketing-Jobs.htm

10 makeuseof.com/tag/top-10-most-effective-job-search-websites/

11 roberthalf.com/job-seekers/career-center/job-hunting-tips/10-of-the-best-job-search-websites

# STEP 4
# APPLICATION STRATEGIES AND TIPS

## QUICK START

The application process can be daunting and overwhelming at times. In order to make the experience less intimidating, you can pursue certain strategies when applying. We have broken up these strategies into four parts:

This chapter presents strategies and tips for applying for entry-level positions. Included are the following:

* An overview of application strategies,
* The advantages and disadvantages of each strategy,
* An in-depth discussion of using your network as an integral part of any application strategy,
* A summary of a recommended "combination" application strategy,
* Principles to guide all communications with your target companies, and
* A sample cover letter applying those communications principles.

## APPLICATION STRATEGIES

### Blast and hope

The blast and hope strategy is more of a shotgun approach. It involves using various job search sites to find as many job opportunities as you can and sending your resume and cover letter to all of them. A benefit of this approach is that it saves the time that would be required to sift through and do a detailed study of individual positions. That said, it is the least efficient at finding a job that is attractive to you. A preferred alternative is to carefully screen positions prior to applying—targeting and subsequently applying only to opportunities that closely align with your dream target position.

## Career center and job fairs

The career center and career/job fairs on your campus provide a great way to find job opportunities. The employers coming to your university are interested in hiring students from your school, a.k.a. *you!* Career fairs can help you begin your job hunt and gain experience applying for jobs, networking and interviewing. Significant preparation is required to be successful at any career/job fair. Researching your target companies and positions ahead of time will pay big dividends.

## Using your connections

The connections in your network can benefit your job search by providing direct access to a wide array of target companies and positions—without an arduous search through career fairs, websites, etc. Your network includes family, co-workers, friends, friends of friends, family friends, professors, contacts from your internships, and recruiters you may know, even the one you met last year at a marketing summit. Your network includes anyone who knows you directly or indirectly and who is willing to help you. The goal is to have someone in your network become your 'sponsor' in order to help you get your foot in the door, off of the huge stack of resumes of candidates, and directly into the interview room.

## A combination: the recommended strategy

Overall, a combination strategy offers the best approach. The more outlets you use to find jobs, the better. Using job search websites, your university's career center resources and job fairs, and your own personal network will open you up to the most opportunities and the largest pool of attractive positions.

# GENERAL APPLICATION TIPS

## Key attitudes to project

In all correspondence and interviews you should try to project certain desirable attitudes. These attitudes include your passion, willingness to take on new opportunities, capacity to succeed no matter what situation you face, and skill in handling setbacks productively. All the while, stay humble and show off your fun, likable personality. These attitudes should permeate every part of your application process, from your resume to your cover letter through all of your interviews.

## Cover letters

We have already touched on resume formatting, and we will discuss interviewing in depth in Step 5, but cover letters are an important component of your application as well. When crafting your cover letters, using a specific format will help you get your message across. Follow this simple framework:

- ❖ *Why them:* Why are you reaching out and why are you interested in this particular company and position?
- ❖ *Why you:* Why should the company be interested in you?
- ❖ *Next steps:* What are the next steps you and the company should take? You should also thank the reader for his/her time and consideration.

## The unavoidable wait

Once you submit your applications, the often frustrating wait begins. Any company has a variety of reasons why it might take some time to get back to you about your application. Be patient, stay positive, and follow up in a timely fashion if you haven't heard anything.

# APPLICATION STRATEGIES

We split application strategies into four approaches and sub-categories of each. The four approaches are:

- ❖ Blast and hope;
- ❖ Career center and job fairs;
- ❖ Using your connections; and
- ❖ The recommended strategy, a combination.

Let's review these strategies and consider the advantages and disadvantages of each. In the end, we will recommend a combination of these options.

# BLAST AND HOPE

## All-out blast and hope strategy

- ❖ Go to Indeed.com or any popular job search site reviewed in Step 3;
- ❖ Search for your target job (e.g., "entry-level marketing jobs in Chicago");
- ❖ Shotgun all of those 400+ opportunities—fill out each application and send your resume and cover letter to all;
- ❖ Then, sit and wait for the job offers to roll in (Don't you wish!).

## More selective blast and hope strategy

Follow the strategy above, but, before applying, quickly screen the 400+ jobs. Use filters (e.g., full-time jobs, a minimum salary) to reduce the 400 to 150 or so.

# Yet more selective strategy

Do a more careful screening than above, reducing your set of relevant opportunities from 150+ down to about 20 or 30 by looking more carefully at all (of the 150+) opportunities and eliminating those that do not meet additional important criteria such as:

- ❖ Type of marketing position (e.g., advertising, research, sales, retail, etc.); or
- ❖ Type of company (**e.g., industry, specific location, company size, etc.**).

# Most selective strategy

Do a much more careful screening, again as Step 3 describes. Of the 20+ jobs remaining, eliminate those that don't pass the following tests:

- ❖ Compare your documented qualifications (from Step 2) with an in-depth look at the job requirements of each of the 20 to 30 remaining positions.
- ❖ Scrutinize each of the remaining 10 to 15 positions with a careful look at the companies' ratings and reviews on Glassdoor.

# Advantages and disadvantages of blast and hope strategies

## Advantages

- ❖ *No need to set your search criteria.* Maybe you don't know what you would like to do and would rather see what's available to help you decide. A blast to hundreds of companies will likely get you at least considered for more positions than a more focused approach.
- ❖ *No study needed.* You won't need to study and evaluate in depth each of the hundreds of prospective positions you are pursuing.
- ❖ *Unanticipated attractive opportunity.* You might receive an invitation to converse and potentially interview with a company you otherwise might have overlooked, dismissed off-hand, or screened out for any reason. There's always a chance such an entry-level position might turn out to be right for you.
- ❖ *Auto-entry onto the 'short stack.'* You might get lucky. Since you have more balls in the air, more recruiters could contact you, putting you directly onto more 'short stacks' of applications that receive closer, more immediate consideration.

## Disadvantages

- ❖ *Time.* Filling out 400 applications takes a great deal of time, which you might better spend very quickly exploring and screening out the jobs that are clearly irrelevant for you given your preferences and qualifications.
- ❖ *Less time available for applications for relevant positions.* Why spend your limited time completing applications for positions that are irrelevant for

you? Spend more time doing a better job on applications for positions that better fit your preferences and qualifications.

❖ *Unattractive opportunities emerge.* If you blast out applications for a host of potential positions, a certain subset of the companies contacting you for consideration will be doing so to discuss positions that are clearly unattractive to you. Do you think you would like a 100 percent commission-based job cold-calling target customers? Perhaps—but more likely, no. This puts you in an awkward situation. You applied, they expressed interest, and now you have to ignore or turn them down. This process wastes time, energy and resources for the companies and for you.

# Advantages and disadvantages of carefully screening positions prior to applying

## Advantages

❖ *Forces self-evaluation.* Eventually you need to spend time considering:
  ❖ Your preferred type (or types) of position, company characteristics, location, salary, etc.; and
  ❖ How well your qualifications line up with your preferences.
❖ *Better applications and better yield.* By quickly screening out less attractive, less relevant positions, you can spend more time and, in turn, do a better job developing and focusing your applications for more attractive, more relevant positions. Logically, these better applications should increase the number of exploratory responses you receive from your more carefully selected set of available positions.
❖ *More attractive exploratory responses.* Because you will have targeted your applications toward more attractive positions, the exploratory responses you do receive are more likely to be for positions that are indeed both attractive and relevant for you.

## Disadvantages

❖ *A more limited universe of potential positions.* Maybe, despite considerable soul-searching, studying Step 1, and perusing other sources describing careers in marketing[1], you do not yet have any marketing position preferences and would rather see what is available to help you decide. A blast to hundreds of companies is likely to get you at least considered for more positions than a more focused approach.
❖ *Significant study time required.* It takes time to screen out (using the filters available in job search engines), click on, explore, and eventually screen out many dozens of the remaining positions that, after further scrutiny, simply aren't attractive or don't line up with your qualifications.

# CAREER CENTER AND JOB FAIRS

As discussed in Step 3, two of the most helpful resources for your job search are your university's career center and job fairs geared specifically toward college students. Two types of job fairs can fall under this category: those your university puts together and those created by an external source. We will focus mainly on fairs your university initiates, but the principles apply to external fairs as well.

## Advantages

❖ *Everything to gain, nothing to lose.* Your campus career center was created for the express purpose of helping its students choose a career, find opportunities, and fine-tune their skills for postgraduate jobs. Career centers provide services such as career aptitude tests, career counseling, alumni connections, excursions to employers' offices, mock interviews, resume and cover letter help, workshops, and much more.[2]

❖ *Potential for employment.* Most companies that attend job fairs want to hire students they meet at the fair. Oftentimes, recruiters will ask students in whom they saw potential to interview later that day or the following day for open positions within the company. Job fairs are a great place to bypass the initial job application and screening process that you would have to go through when applying to positions online. This step in interviewing is often the most difficult to get past!

❖ *Industry exposure and networking.* Freshmen and sophomores will find plenty of opportunities, too. A career fair offers a chance to meet industry professionals and begin building your network. Hearing the skill sets and qualifications required for specific companies and positions can help you determine the career path you'd like to take. Not only that, but talking with recruiters and industry professionals will also give you connections you can utilize down the road when you are looking for a position.

❖ *Great experience for building confidence.* Job fairs are the perfect place to practice behaving in a professional setting. Interacting with industry professionals can feel foreign at first, but conversations at job fairs oftentimes resemble future interviews for positions and, as such, can help prepare you for your future interviews.[3]

## Disadvantages

❖ *Limited pool of employers.* One setback of career center connections and job fairs is that there are only so many businesses with which one university can be closely connected. Over time, universities and employers form relationships through previous visits, alumni holding positions within the company, and positive experiences on both the university's side and the employer's side of past hires. With more than 29 million small businesses and 18,000 larger firms in the United States,[4] there's no way your university has connections with all of them. So, if you want to work for specific companies with which your career center is not closely connected, then you will need another strategy to get your foot in the door.

❖ *Regional shortcomings.* Many times, collegiate career centers and job fairs draw employers from the surrounding areas. This is mainly due to the fact that recruiters are more likely to attend job fairs and interview on campus if the travel expenses aren't high. This isn't to say that all of the attendees to a career fair or all of the positions on a career center job portal will be from one geographic area. Overall, however, companies from far way places are less likely to participate in the Career Fair at your school.

❖ *Overwhelming if unprepared.* Career fairs are arranged so students can wander from one booth to the next. This setup calls for an open area with a large crowd of applicants trying to get the attention and interest of participating companies and interviewers. If you've never attended a career fair before or spoken to someone (a career center advisor, for example) about a strategy, then the event can be very overwhelming. The key is to research the companies you like ahead of time and go in with a plan. The more prepared you come, the less stressful and more productive your experience will be.

# USING YOUR CONNECTIONS: NETWORKING

Let's step back a bit. The advice provided in the earlier steps should help you prepare materials that will give you a better chance of advancing in the evaluation and interview process once you get a recruiter's initial attention and careful consideration. Given the competitiveness of most entry-level positions today, however, one of the biggest challenges is to get recruiters' attention in the first place and to then somehow encourage them to carefully consider you and your materials. This is where your network is key.

## Save the DIY approach for your hobbies.

As nice as it would be to get your dream job totally on your own, a commitment to "do-it-yourself" job searching tends to be self-defeating for new college graduates. Others want to help you, and most recent grads just starting out can certainly use some assistance from parents, relatives, friends, professors or virtually anyone who is 'connected' in any way to a targeted company and/or position.

At the same time, keep in mind that while others can get you access to more job opportunities, actually landing the job will depend upon your background, materials, and ability to effectively communicate your qualifications to recruiters.

## Why is networking so important?

Recruiters simply do not have the time, patience, or resources necessary to carefully review each and every resume and application submitted. Experience dictates that they set high initial screening criteria. For entry-level positions, these might include factors such as internship experience, documented in-school leadership experiences, specific courses, GPA, school attended, and perhaps a few others. Using these filters enables recruiters to quickly reduce a huge group of prospective candidates down to a much smaller set— "the short stack" of applicants—with minimal danger of overlooking the best candidates.[5]

If your full range of your materials communicating your credentials clearly stand out from those of the majority of candidates, then, all on your own, you have a strong chance of making the short stack of applications to receive much more careful consideration. Good for you!

Most candidates for most entry-level marketing positions, however, simply do not have the stellar credentials and experiences to make the short stack. Recruiters will, therefore, weed out most candidates quickly with very brief consideration at best and with few (if any) interview opportunities.

This is where networking comes in. Having someone recommend you—someone affiliated either directly or indirectly with a targeted company—can move you immediately into that short stack, even if you do not have the overwhelmingly impressive credentials that would normally be required for you to get more careful consideration on your own.

## How can someone in your network help you?

* *Make you aware of available positions.* Your contacts can make you aware of specific, appropriate positions available either in their own companies or, perhaps, in others. This insight can prove very helpful, particularly if the relevant position has not yet been posted within the company or for the public at large.
* *Sponsor you for identified positions.* Just as importantly, your network can help once you have identified a specific available position at a target company. The best contact in this case is someone (anyone in the list below) who works directly for the targeted company.
* *Help you find a sponsor for target positions.* Your next-best contact is someone with a less direct affiliation—the person who "has a close friend who works there." This person should be willing to adopt and introduce you to an influential contact at the target company.

## Who is in your network?

Your network includes your mother, your father, sister, brother, aunts, uncles, and other near or distant relatives, coworkers, professors, alumni from your college or university, former or current employers, anyone at the career center at your school, personal friends, friends of friends, family friends, friends of family friends, former or current classmates, former or current teammates, a person for whom you caddie at the country club or for whom you babysit or babysat long ago, your neighbors, friends of neighbors—anyone who knows you directly or indirectly and who will willingly help you. Most people like to help others, especially to help young friends or acquaintances who are just starting their careers.

## Constantly build your network.

❖ *Get out there and meet marketing experts every chance you get.* Join online events and forums and contribute. Go to lectures and conferences in your college or city. Stay engaged when you attend. Go to learn, connect, share, and contribute where you can—not to look for a job.

❖ *Get over yourself.* Approach and introduce yourself to key speakers. Comment on and/or inquire about specific points they made. And—here's the key to adding that professional to your network—get a business card or email address and immediately follow up with a brief message making a specific observation pertinent to any particular point made by your new contact. Ask to connect on LinkedIn. Network for the sake of networking.[6]

## If possible, avoid applying until you have a 'sponsor' from your network.

If you apply online without a network sponsor, you automatically go onto the 'big stack' and you might be quickly screened out. Even if, later on, a sponsor intervenes on your behalf, you already have one strike against you. Your sponsor will have to talk your application out of the rejection pile.

If a deadline is not imminent, therefore, delay formally applying as long as possible, until a contact has agreed to sponsor you for your targeted position.

What if you don't have a sponsor? Try to find one using some of the tips below. Start by recognizing the vast array of folks in your network who could sponsor you and help you to automatically make the 'short stack.'

### Alumni employed at your target company are great potential sponsors

Many graduates of your college or university would gladly sponsor you at their companies if they know about you and if an appropriate position is available. Your first challenge is finding those alumni. Contact your career center and the alumni association in your target city to check for alums working at your target company. Get on LinkedIn and use the screening tool to input your school name. Once you have identified a relevant alum:

❖ Send that person a very brief e-mail indicating you have identified a relevant open position at their company.

❖ Include the relevant URL promoting the position so your contact can look it up to see if it still available and to find out who is in the hiring hierarchy for that particular position.

❖ Ask if the person would be willing to communicate with you about the position (face-to-face is by far the best, but not necessary, if inconvenient).

❖ More specifically, ask if she/he would be willing to look over your credentials (e.g., your resume), give you an opinion on whether you are qualified for the position, and, assuming you are qualified, ask what strategy the person would suggest for you to apply for that position

You hope that she/he will "adopt" you and submit your credentials directly to an influential person in the hiring hierarchy for the position. In most instances, that will get you and your credentials on the short stack from the get-go.

## What if you can't identify a potential sponsor at your target company?

This could happen for any number of reasons. Perhaps your target company itself is small, with few employees and, therefore, few potential sponsors. Perhaps it is in a geographic area where your network is sparse. Perhaps you have identified a potential sponsor in the relevant company but have not successfully connected with her/him on LinkedIn—without this connection, it can be difficult to find contact information for a potential sponsor.

### Use your network to find a sponsor.
One strategy is asking for help from someone in your network who has significant experience and an impressive LinkedIn profile. That person will typically have well over 500 first-level and 200,000 to 500,000 or more second-level connections. Given all those contacts and a strong profile, she or he is much more likely than you to know or have access to an appropriate sponsor for you at your target company. An executive of a larger company or an experienced professor might fit the bill here.

For example, a professor who knows you pretty well might have a continuing relationship with a former student and/or with a business professional at your target company. In this instance, your professor would typically already have the potential sponsor's email address and could drop a quick note reading something like this:

> "Greetings once again, Lisa,
>     I hope you are doing well personally and professionally.
>     Say, Lisa, I have a bright and energetic senior, Sally Sample, who is about to graduate. She is interested in exploring a promoted entry-level marketing position at *XYZ Company (include link to the job posting)*.
>     Would you be willing to communicate with Sally about her potential suitability for this position and, if you think she is qualified, perhaps counsel her on a good strategy for applying?
>
> *Thanks much—keep in touch,*
> Jack
> Professor of Marketing

*ABC* University"

As a favor to her former professor, Lisa will likely respond with something like this:

"Certainly! I would happily talk with Sally. Have her drop me an email along with her resume and we can set up a time to chat."

Hopefully, Lisa and Sally will have a cordial and productive conversation that results in Lisa adopting Sally. Lisa would then enthusiastically volunteer to forward Sally's credentials to the appropriate parties in her company, tagging them for special consideration (i.e., the short stack!). Does this happen? Certainly—in fact, all the time!

Why would Lisa go to all that trouble? She might have a number of potential reasons:
- ❖ As a favor to her professor;
- ❖ As a favor to Sally as a fellow alumna and, if their conversation went well, as a new friend;
- ❖ Because people like to help young people get started;
- ❖ Because Lisa's company is always looking for excellent candidates (assuming that Sally falls into that category); and, finally,
- ❖ When Lisa sponsors a candidate and that person makes it through the evaluation process, joins the firm, and becomes a productive new employee, Lisa gets a new feather in her cap. All companies want good people. Recommended candidates help shorten the hiring process—a boon for any company—and have a higher probability of turning out to be quality performers. For those reasons, some companies even provide financial rewards (several thousands of dollars in some instances) to employees who recommend and "tag" candidates they ultimately hire— yet another potential incentive for Lisa to help Sally.

### When no one you know has a contact, you should:

First, check the school tab on LinkedIn to see if you can find a graduate at your target company. If so, you could try to connect with that person on LinkedIn, and they might respond and offer to look over your materials, make some suggestions, and potentially sponsor you for the targeted position by tagging and/or submitting your materials for you.

Another potentially more successful alternative, once you have identified an alumna or alumnus, is approaching someone in your network who is highly experienced and has a strong, well-crafted LinkedIn profile. Ask that person if they could try to get that alum to communicate with you. A professor, for example, might write a note similar to the one above:[7]

*"Hello Lisa (the target sponsor),*

*I have a bright and energetic senior, Sally Sample, who is about to graduate. She is interested in exploring a promoted entry level marketing position at XYZ Company (include link to the job posting). Would you be willing to communicate with Sally about her potential suitability for this position and, if you think she is qualified, perhaps counsel her on a good strategy for applying for that position?*

*Thanks very much for your consideration.*

*Jack Reynolds*
*Professor of Marketing*
*ABC University"*

In this instance, since Lisa of XYZ Company does not know your professor, she will likely check out the professor's profile on LinkedIn before deciding whether to respond. Once she sees a strong, seasoned profile from a professor from her own college or university, she will probably respond, inviting the referred student (you) to communicate with her.

You can use the same approach—having an experienced member of your network make the initial contact for you—even if neither you nor anyone else in your network (e.g., your professor) can identify anyone working at the company who is also a graduate of your college or university.[8] In this instance, you are hoping that the strength of your professor's profile itself will encourage Lisa to respond positively.

Lisa is less likely to respond to your professor and invite you to communicate with her if she is not a graduate. In such instances, therefore, it would make sense to ask your professor to send the initial request to more than a single person in the target company. Help your professor out by scanning LinkedIn for several target sponsors, and sharing links to their profiles with your professor.

# Examples

As emphasized above, your network can help you get noticed in a crowded field of more or less equally qualified candidates. Consider these additional scenarios.

* ❖ Someone with whom you have worked (e.g., in an internship) can endorse you with specific praises, emphasizing your key relevant strengths.
* ❖ Other recommenders might only know you socially, but they still might provide a direct link to an influential person in the recruiting hierarchy.
* ❖ Someone you know could be part of the recruiting hierarchy and might be able to get you directly into the short stack of applications, as a favor to you or as a favor to one of their colleagues on your behalf.
* ❖ Others in your network might have no direct affiliation with a target company but might have important business contacts at that company.
* ❖ Yet others, perhaps a professor, might receive requests for competitive candidates from former colleagues or former students now working at the target company.

# RECOMMENDED APPLICATION STRATEGY: A COMBINATION

Given the advantages and disadvantages of the strategies presented above, we recommend simultaneously pursuing a variety of these approaches. By doing so, you can reap the rewards of each approach and minimize the various drawbacks. For the most productive use of this method, adhere to the following principles:

## First is not last.

As emphasized in Step 3, when you start applying for positions, remember that your first position will not be your last and it is highly unlikely that any first job will meet all of your preferences and expectations. Gaining some real-world experience should be the overriding goal of your first position.

## Be proactive in using your network.

Assume that most folks in your network like you and want to help you. Let them do so by engaging with them. Let them know what you are looking for and actively following up on any leads they provide. Leads from those in your network who have direct affiliations with your specific companies of interest hold the greatest potential. Refer back to the many additional tips provided above for leveraging your network in your search for an attractive entry-level position.

## Explore all inquiries from recruiters.

Energetically and punctually follow up on any feelers you receive from recruiters who contact you based upon their scan of your LinkedIn profile, your resume that you dropped at a job fair, or the like. At minimum, find out more about each specific recruiter inquiry to determine whether the prospective position is consistent with your preferences and qualifications.

## Actively explore positions you find in job search engines.

If you are active with your network and in job fairs, it is highly possible that your first position will materialize through one contact or another gained through such exposure. But you cannot count on that. It also makes total sense to regularly scour the Internet for alternative opportunities.

As reviewed in Step 3, start by Googling "entry-level marketing jobs," and enter any of the multiple job search engines that pop up, such as Indeed, Simply Hired, LinkedIn, Career Rookie, Monster, and many others. Within any one or several of these job search engines:

❖ First, enter "entry-level marketing position" plus your desired location in the site's search box;

❖ Use the site's filters to narrow down alternatives prior to clicking on and actually exploring individual opportunities;

❖ Scroll through the opportunities to view the position titles, dismissing any that obviously do not fit your position and company preferences;

❖ Start clicking on the remaining set of opportunities, quickly scanning each and again eliminating any that are obviously a poor fit;

❖ Boil down your list to 20 to 30 opportunities to explore in greater depth;

❖ Examine those opportunities more carefully, striving to identify a subset of 5 to 10 with the greatest potential for you (i.e., that are most consistent with your preferences and qualifications) and proceed by:

    ❖ Studying the **job description and job requirements** for each position. Prioritize those that fit you best; and

    ❖ Double checking and excluding **positions no longer available** (this happens quite often, as some companies tend to dally in taking down opportunities once filled).

    ❖ Checking **the Glassdoor ratings** for each company. For any with marginal ratings (e.g., fewer than 70 percent would recommend the company to a friend or fewer than 80 percent approve of the CEO), check the sample size of reviews and, if adequate, carefully read a representative group of both the good and bad reviews.

❖ Weigh the remaining 5 to 10 well-screened, highly prioritized listings:

    ❖ **Rank order them** and examine the highest priority ones first;

    ❖ Use strategies suggested earlier in this chapter to **get an in-company sponsor for each** prioritized position;

    ❖ Then, if at all possible, **apply through your in-company sponsor** to improve your chances of making the short stack, where you and your materials will receive careful scrutiny, hopefully leading to interview opportunities.

# NEXT UP: FORMULATING
# YOUR APPLICATION

If you submitted your materials through an in-company sponsor, as discussed and advised above, then the chances of your materials getting a careful look rises significantly. Great! That said, this first step by no means dictates that you will automatically move forward in the evaluation and interview process. Your resume and background material content must be strong. Just as importantly as that content, however, will be *the attitudes you project* in your correspondence, your materials, and your interviews.

Next we describe a number of key attitudes that, if projected, can move you to the front of the line of candidates applying for any position.

# ATTITUDES TO PROJECT

## Passion

Always exude passion and enthusiasm. Passiveness is a deal-breaker—passion is key. If you don't get excited about your own personal and professional interests and accomplishments, the employer will think, "She or he will never get excited about working with us, and we don't need apathy around here."

## Confidence in uncharted territory

Emphasize that you are not only open to but anxious to take on areas wholly unfamiliar to you. Clearly communicate that you recognize taking on new challenges as the best way to learn, to expand your own experiences and qualifications, and to become a more productive employee and team member. You enthusiastically embrace the new and unknown. You are clever. You are self-confident. You relish the challenge of figuring out new and better ways to do anything. Provide examples of how you have done this in the past and emphasize the related benefits.

## Can-do attitude

Clearly communicate that you are accustomed to succeeding and making things work out, no matter what challenges you face. Describe situations in which your glass-half-full mentality improved or saved a project. Provide examples.

## Humble enthusiasm

Respect the fine line between arrogance and enthusiasm. Arrogance boasts that you have clearly proven your qualifications, merit, and obvious fit for the job. Enthusiasm communicates openness, eagerness, and passion, demonstrating your desire to take on and excel in the relevant position. Arrogance is a turn-off, while enthusiasm is a turn-on.

## Resilience in turning setbacks into successes

Express, with examples, that you can humbly admit to and take responsibility for temporary failures. Indicate how, simultaneously, you maintain your can-do attitude and always commit to expending full effort to turn failures into eventual successes.

## Easygoingness

Exude your fun side and sense of humor, especially in face-to-face interviews. Don't take yourself too seriously. Casually relating (with a smile on your face) self-effacing stories of moments from your past—in academic, social, or business situations—can provide a vehicle for projecting your personality and your ability to make and take a joke. Who doesn't like to work with fun people? They help make everyone's day more enjoyable.

# YOUR COVER LETTER

## Guiding principles

- ❖ Submit your cover letter and other materials through an in-company sponsor whenever possible.
- ❖ Get right to your primary qualifications.
- ❖ Quantify your qualifications.
- ❖ Be brief—limit your letter to a page if possible.
- ❖ Do not be presumptuous.
- ❖ Readily offer access to additional information.
- ❖ Invite a timely response.
- ❖ Include a cordial close.

## The format of your cover letter

When writing your cover letter, having a planned, simple format can help you start and structure your message. Your cover letter should include three parts:[9]

- ❖ *Why them?* The first paragraph should detail your reason for writing this employer. Further, it should plainly express why you are interested in and applying to the particular company. You will improve the quality of your content if you conduct prior research on the company, marketing efforts they've had, and campaigns they've conducted to show you are truly knowledgeable about and interested in the particular company. You should reference any sponsors you have at the company in this paragraph.

- ❖ *Why you?* The second paragraph argues why the company should hire you. This is your chance to show off your qualifications through relating a few experiences. Your 'leadership stories' (from Step #2) provide a great place to find content for this paragraph—you should use them to indirectly prove that your background is a great match for the relevant position. Close with a confident sentence summarizing your skills and affirming you can contribute to the organization – while referring to your relevant background.

- ❖ *Next steps?* To finalize your cover letter, close with a third paragraph discussing what you want to happen next—this might be an interview, a conversation about employment opportunities, or an opportunity to further discuss your qualifications. Additionally, within this paragraph you can reference your attached resume, thank the person and indicate that you look forward to hearing from or speaking with him/her.

## Examples:

In this example, for simplicity's sake, we assume a hard-copy application and resume submission. The same principles would apply to a slightly adapted cover letter accompanying an online application, which is more common today.

Sydney Albright is graduating from the University of Illinois in May 20xx with a degree in marketing. She is applying for an entry-level assistant marketing analyst position at XYZ Company.

## Situation 1:

Sydney shotguns her letter and materials to XYZ Company. She has **no contacts or in-company sponsor** at XYZ.

---

Sydney Albright
Urbana, IL 61801-4788
Cell: 573-262-xxxx
e-mail: salbright@illinois.edu

February 1, 20XX
HR Department
XYZ Company

Greetings XYZ Recruiters,

My name is Sydney Albright, and this May I will graduate from the University of Illinois. I am currently searching for a challenging entry-level marketing position.

Since I am particularly interested in pursuing a career in marketing analytics, your promoted entry-level Assistant Marketing Analyst position (JRU29715 —*add URL here*) sparked my interest, and I would like to apply for that position

My background includes:
* A marketing degree from the U. of Illinois, with a minor in applied mathematics (3.62 overall GPA);
* A three-month summer internship (summer 20xx) learning and applying Search Engine Optimization models with MNOP advertising agency in Chicago. I worked under MNOP's SEO Director, applying their optimization model to help seven different companies improve their organic rankings from an average of 45th to 8th, with four of the seven websites making it to the first page of Google;
* A four day in-person course in summer 20xx on Marketing Analytics and Consumer Insights from the Direct Marketing Association; and
* Online Web-Analytics Certification (Dec. 20xx), earned over a four-week period in Fall 20xx from the OnLineMarketingInstitute.org.

I would be delighted to communicate with you or anyone else at XYZ to provide more information on my background and experiences and, hopefully, to explore my potential suitability for the Assistant Marketing Analyst position.

Please let me know if you or anyone else at XYZ might like any additional information. Three references are included in my resume.

Thank you very much for your time and interest.

Sincerely,
Sydney Albright
University of Illinois 20xx Marketing Graduate
Attachment: Sydney Albright Resume and References

---

## Situation 2:

Sydney **does not have an in-company sponsor, but she met XYZ recruiter** Ronald Housman at a career fair just yesterday. Mr. Housman is a casual acquaintance at this point and has not agreed to sponsor Sydney. He did, however, encourage Sydney to send an e-mail letter and resume directly to him.

---

Greetings Mr. Housman,

It was pleasure to meet you yesterday at the University of Illinois Career Fair. As you suggested, along with this note of introduction I am attaching my resume and application for the XYZ entry-level Assistant Marketing Analyst position currently appearing in the career opportunities section of your website (*URL*).

This coming May, I will receive my degree from the University of Illinois. Currently I am searching for a challenging entry level marketing position. I am particularly interested in pursuing a career in marketing analytics, which is why the XYZ position caught my eye.

My background includes:

❖ A marketing major at the U. of Illinois with a minor in applied mathematics (3.62 overall GPA);
❖ A three-month summer internship (summer 20xx) learning and applying Search Engine Optimization models with MNOP advertising agency in Chicago. I worked under MNOP's SEO Director, applying their optimization model to help seven different companies improve their organic rankings from an average of 45th to 8th, with four of the seven websites making it to the first page of Google;
❖ A four day in-person course in summer 20xx on Marketing Analytics and Consumer Insights from the Direct Marketing Association; and
❖ Online Web-Analytics Certification (Dec. 20xx), earned over a four-week period in Fall 20xx from OnLineMarketingInstitute.org

I would be delighted to communicate with you or anyone else at XYZ to provide more information on my background and experiences and, hopefully, to explore my potential suitability for the Assistant Marketing Analyst position.

Please let me know if you or anyone else at XYZ would like any additional information. Three references are included in my resume.

Thank you very much for your time and interest.

Sincerely,
Sydney Albright
University of Illinois 20XX Marketing Graduate
Attachment: Sydney Albright Resume and References

## Situation 3:

Sydney **has an in-company sponsor**, Ms. Ruth Garner, an Illinois alumna, who has communicated several times with Sydney, agreeing to help her in her quest for a marketing position at XYZ. Ms. Garner asked Sydney to submit her letter of introduction, application, and resume directly to her. Hopefully, she will pass Sydney's materials directly on to the pre-screened short stack of applications.

---

Greetings once again, Ms. Garner,

It has been a pleasure communicating with you. Thank you very much for your time, effort, and suggestions as I take the first steps in starting my marketing career.

As requested, along with this letter of introduction, I am attaching my resume and my application for the XYZ entry-level Assistant Marketing Analyst position currently appearing in the career opportunities section of your website (*URL*).

Reviewing our discussion, this coming May I will graduate from the University of Illinois. Currently I am searching for a challenging entry-level marketing position. I have a particular interest in marketing analytics, which is why the XYZ position caught my eye.

My background includes:

❖ A marketing major with a minor in applied mathematics (3.62 overall GPA);
❖ A three-month summer internship (summer 20xx) applying Search Engine Optimization models with MNOP advertising agency in Chicago. I worked under MNOP's SEO Director, applying their optimization model to help seven different companies improve their organic rankings from an average of 45th to 8th, with four of the seven websites making it to the first page of Google;
❖ A four day in-person course in summer 20xx on Marketing Analytics and Consumer Insights from the Direct Marketing Association; and
❖ Online Web-Analytics Certification (Dec. 20xx), earned over a four-week period in Fall 20xx from OnLineMarketingInstitute.org

I would be delighted to communicate further with you or anyone else at XYZ to provide more information on my background and experiences and, hopefully, to explore my potential suitability for the Assistant Marketing Analyst position.

Please let me know if you or anyone else at XYZ might like any additional information. Three references are included in my resume.

Thank you very much for your time and interest.

Sincerely,

Sydney Albright
University of Illinois 20XX Marketing Graduate
Attachment: Sydney Albright Resume and References

# THE WAITING GAME

Assume you just applied for a position, like Sydney above. Assume also that you attended to the suggestions and caveats throughout this book. For example:

- ❖ You did your homework on the prospective company and position ahead of time. You like the "sound" of this particular position and feel that your resume and materials qualify you for the position (Step 1).
- ❖ You have adhered to the principles for formatting and crafting your resume and supporting materials (Step 2).
- ❖ Your communications in your correspondence and application itself reflect the positive attitudes outlined in this chapter.

Now you wait. Applying for any position is stressful for virtually anyone. Keep that in mind—you will experience normal anxiety, and you are not alone. It's difficult, but in the short term, the best strategy is to sit on your hands for that particular application and get to work on your next one.

But the wait continues. You don't understand, as the deadline for applications is now long past. Why did they not contact you? All sorts of scenarios might be going on, with a nearly endless list of reasons that could keep you waiting.

## Why haven't I heard back?

Professionals are very busy people. Reducing your stress is very, very low on their priority lists. You might be among their very top candidates, but:

- ❖ Some very pressing issues unrelated to this position may have come up, delaying the recruiters' efforts to immediately fill this particular position.
- ❖ The need for this position might have disintegrated with the loss of a key client, a merger, or new dictates from above to hold or cut headcount.
- ❖ You may be a solid candidate, but they may have first offered the position to someone else perceived as slightly better qualified. They are waiting for an acceptance or rejection from that person. This other person receiving the offer may herself have put this company's offer on hold, waiting for another potentially more attractive offer from a totally different company. Yes, this is frustrating. But if the person with the offer rejects it, you may be next up to get that offer. Stay positive!

## What do I do if I don't hear anything?

Again, stay positive! Most applications have a specific deadline (usually indicated in the job guidelines). If you haven't heard back within one week after the deadline has passed, it is time to act. If you let it linger, what will the company think about your genuine interest in the prospective position?

Wait a week after the deadline and then send a short email to your original contact—the same channel you originally used for submitting your application—or to a new contact you may have received earlier from a person acknowledging receipt of your application. Be sure your original contact also receives a copy of your follow-up note (if you are reaching out to someone else).

In this short follow-up note, once again enthusiastically express your interest in the prospective position and inquire about when you can expect to hear back. At the bottom of your note, include the e-mail thread to any acknowledgement you have received as well as the thread of your original cover letter. Attach your resume again, too. The thread and resume attachment will save the reader the time and trouble of digging up your original information. This, in turn, can speed any potential response and update from the recipient.

# Example:

> *"Greetings once again, XYZ Recruiters (or your individual recruiter, Ronald Housman, or your sponsor, Ruth Garner, or anyone who may have acknowledged receipt of your application),*
>
> *Back on mm/dd/yy I formally applied for the entry-level Assistant Marketing Analyst position (include job code and/or URL). I wonder if you could please update me on where I stand in the application process.*
>
> *My strong interest in that position continues, and I would enthusiastically pursue any opportunity to discuss my background and potential suitability for the position with anyone at XYZ.*
>
> *Thank you very much for your time and consideration. I look forward to hearing from you.*
> *Sincerely,*
> *Sydney Albright*
> *University of Illinois 20xx Marketing Graduate*
> *Attachment: Sydney Albright Resume and References"*

# Be aware: the waiting game for agencies

When applying to advertising, media, or public relations agencies, the waiting game can be different than those of other companies. There is much more fluidity within agencies as they frequently gain and lose clients. Agencies tend to hire when the demand for more employees increases because of newly attained clients. They will often interview candidates for entry-level positions that they hope to open in the future. This way, when they need to hire more employees, they already have a group of pre-interviewed candidates ready to bring on board.

The downside of this process for you, the interviewee, is that the agency might want to hire you, but they might not have work available or a spot available right now. As a result, you might be stuck in a position in which you have to search for alternative positions with other companies. Alternatively, if you are patient and very self-confident, you can stay in close communications with your key contact at the initially targeted agency and get a feel for whether and when a position and offer might be available for you.

Lesson. Don't get your heart set on getting an offer from a specific agency. The agency may love you and your qualifications, but may simply not have a position open for you. So keep your options open by actively seeking more than a single position.

## Step #4 REVIEW QUESTIONS

1. Describe the Blast & Hope Strategy.
2. What are the benefits of carefully screening positions rather than using Blast & Hope?
3. List three advantages and disadvantages of using your school's career center resources.
4. Describe three ways that someone in your network can help you in the job search.
5. True or False: You can always count on your network to find you a job. Elaborate.
6. List and describe attitudes that you should project during all correspondence and interviews for any job.
7. What are the key components to include in your application cover letter?
8. Indicate several reasons why, even after interviewing at the company, you may have to wait weeks, or even months before hearing back from a prospective employer.
9. How long should you wait before following up if you haven't heard back after an interview? What should you do / say when you do get back to your contact at the company?
10. Describe the waiting game for agency positions. Why is it unique? What 'wait' strategy should you be prepared to implement?

---

1 For example, Careers in Marketing – Eric Siebert (2016) – Amazon, Create-Space

2 fastweb.com/career-planning/articles/benefits-of-college-career-centers

3 linkedin.com/pulse/importance-attending-job-fair-training-expo-rais-iqbal-2

4 sba.gov/sites/default/files/FAQ_Sept_2012.pdf

5 Some companies use any of a large number of available resume or application screening software programs (at times referred to as "resume robots'") that look for keywords (positive) and certain history (red flags) to screen in and screen out candidates. You can research these on the Internet all day, e.g., the nature of and ways to beat such programs. The bottom line is, if you have stellar credentials and materials, you are more likely to survive the initial screening than if you do not.

6 twistimage.com/blog/archives/8-ways-to-score-that-elusive-entry-level-marketing-position/
For more networking tips, see Never Eat Alone by Keith Ferrazzi.

7 For your network contact to communicate with someone he or she is not 'Connected' with on LinkedIn, your network contact can either request to be Connected, or, can use LinkedIn's In-Mail feature (available to those with a premium LinkedIn account).

8 It is possible that a graduate from your college does work at XYZ Company. but doesn't show up on LinkedIn because he or she does not have a complete or public LinkedIn profile. Check with the Career Center at your college to see if they know of any alumni working at XYZ. You should always target alumni whenever possible to improve your chances of securing an internal sponsor.

9 careercenter.nd.edu/students/resumes-and-cover-letters/cover-letters/

# STEP 5
# INTERVIEW STRATEGIES
# AND TIPS

## QUICK START

Step 5 provides insight into the interview process. Confidence is essential, and you need to prepare properly to interview well. This chapter details all topics related to interviewing, from tips to different situations you might encounter to the various kinds of interviews tactics and techniques.

Note these 13 important interviewing tips.

- ❖ **Anticipate, prepare, and practice introductory interview questions.**
- ❖ **Make your first impression count.**
- ❖ **Relax and have fun.**
- ❖ **Show your passion and enthusiasm.**
- ❖ **Have your leadership stories ready.**
- ❖ **Project your curiosity.**
- ❖ **Don't be afraid to say, "I don't know."**
- ❖ **Don't be afraid to "interview" the interviewer.**
- ❖ **Use your wrap-up question.**
- ❖ **Demonstrate your social skills.**
- ❖ **Prepare for group interviews.**
- ❖ **Follow up with each employee you met.**
- ❖ **Demonstrate desirable attitudes.**

Aside from these tips, remember to keep and display the kind of positive attitude we discussed in Step 4 through all aspects of the interview. The interviews themselves can occur in many formats—in-person on campus, in-person company visits, or Skype—that will all vary in length. Many times, elements of the interviews change as you go through the process, from their tone to the number of interviewers, to the positions held by your interviewers.

When it comes to the content of the interview itself, we discuss several kinds of interview questions you may be asked. These include:

* Introductory questions
* Behavioral questions
* Situational questions
* Critical thinking questions
* Off-the-wall, oddball questions

Overall, each category necessitates its own kind of preparation. Some positions will focus more on one category than another. Doing investigative searching online through websites like Glassdoor can help you prepare for the specific questions the employer might ask.

As we have stated earlier, following up after every round of interviewing is essential if you want to be a priority candidate they truly consider. These follow-ups should express gratitude and demonstrate personalization to every individual with whom you spoke. Distinguish your letters by having specific points of reference from the interviews.

# GENERAL INTERVIEW TIPS

Beyond preparing and practicing, review these tips garnered from in-depth discussions with experienced interviewers from General Mills, AT&T, IBM, Gallo, Nielsen, Target and a variety of other companies. We will go into detail on some of these important suggestions.

* **Anticipate, prepare, and practice introductory interview questions.**
* **Make your first impression count.**
* **Relax and have fun.**
* **Show your passion and enthusiasm.**
* **Have your leadership stories ready.**
* **Project your curiosity.**
* **Don't be afraid to say, "I don't know."**
* **Don't be afraid to "interview" the interviewer.**
* **Use your wrap-up question.**
* **Demonstrate your social skills.**
* **Prepare for group interviews.**
* **Follow up with each employee you met.**
* **Demonstrate desirable attitudes.**

# THIRTEEN POINTS TO REMEMBER

## Anticipate, prepare, and practice.

In many first interview situations you may have only a minute or so to make your first, lasting impression. It is natural to be nervous in this situation. Despite that nervousness, you need to immediately project self-confidence and maturity if you hope to spark the interviewer's interest enough to be invited to the next round of interviews.

***The best way to get over nervousness is to prepare for and practice your answers for anticipated questions.*** Prepare carefully. Practice again and again with friends, family, and/or career center counselors. The better you prepare and the more you practice, the less nervous you will be and the higher the probability that you will be able to project the professionalism that will differentiate you from other, less prepared applicants.[1]

Later in the chapter, we provide a list of specific questions to prepare and practice for first interviews for any entry-level marketing position.

## MAKE YOUR FIRST IMPRESSION COUNT.

When you first walk in the door and find the hiring manager, you have about 90 seconds to impress her. Your first impression is incredibly important. As the (very true) saying goes, "You never get a second chance to make a first impression." So, make it count. Dress for success—you cannot overdress! Be the best-dressed person in line at the career fair. Make immediate eye contact while smiling and giving a firm handshake. Use body language throughout the conversation to communicate your professionalism—attend to your posture, avoid crossing your arms (which can suggest boredom or lack of interest), never look at your phone or watch. Communicate with your voice, body language, and comments that you are extremely interested in the interviewer, the company, and the position.

## Relax and have fun.

Don't try to be someone you are not. You are meeting a new person. If you have prepared and present a professional image, you can relax. Lighten up. Don't take yourself so seriously. Show your self-confidence. Smile, look, and act like you have been there before and are having fun!

## Show your passion and enthusiasm.

People like to hire and hang out with people who are enthusiastic, fun, and passionate. If you are not excited about your own personal interests and accomplishments, or about the prospective position for which you are interviewing, the employer will think you will never get excited about working with the company. Prospective employers want enthusiastic doers, take-by-the-horns folks who meet failures head-on and turn them into success, people who radiate passion and get others excited about new ideas—new ideas on anything!

## Have your leadership stories ready.

Prepare to answer interviewers who are unprepared for you, who will invariably ask, "Tell me/us about yourself," or "Walk me/us through your resume." Jump right to your stories. Each story should have a clear and concise message: "Here was the situation. Here was the challenge. Here's the action I (or we) took. Here was the result (including a numerical change whenever possible). Here is what I learned from this." Use a balance of stories from school (academic, athletic, social) and from work (internships or other work experiences).

## Project your curiosity.

Companies love curiosity in prospective hires—show this through your questions.

- *Make well-thought-out inquiries*—both planned and responsive questions—throughout your individual or group interviews, but don't ask one question after another without carefully listening to the interviewer's response. After the interviewer's response, try to ask a natural follow-up question to make it obvious that you are a good listener.
- *Carefully prepare some questions ahead of time to ask your interviewers*. Google search the company name and read (in depth) articles about the company a day or two before the interview. Prepare and write down several very relevant questions about:

  - Situations the company is currently facing (current sales trends, new clients, new areas of the company's business, the company's products and services, etc.);
  - The industry in general; and
  - The company's primary competitors and the ways that the company differentiates itself from them.

- *Prepare a few questions about the economy, markets, and the world in general* to demonstrate that you keep up with the news. Start reading the general news *now*. Focus on the business world so you can talk about current global and domestic events and trends. This will sharpen your business language and attest to your general savvy.

## Don't be afraid to say, "I don't know."

You aren't expected to know all of the specifics in the industry or the company's products/services, competitors, target customers, etc.—you just need to know enough to have an intelligent conversation. One technique to deflect difficult questions is to say, "I am not sure, but I would love to take a moment to write it down so I can look up more info on this, as sounds really interesting," or something similar. An interested response is always better than saying, 'I don't know.'

# Don't be afraid to "interview" the interviewer.

Ask questions like:

* ❖ "Why do you like working for XYZ?"—that's a great way to break the ice. Plus, you might be able to use their answer again later in the conversation;
* ❖ "How did you get started here?" or, "What/Which do you think is the best place/position to start?";
* ❖ "What is a typical career path for new hires in this position, say, over a five-year period, assuming they are successful?"

## USE YOUR WRAP-UP QUESTION.

As you sense the second or final interview is nearing an end, whether you have a good or bad feeling about how the interview has gone, consider asking outright:

*"What concerns do you have about me relating to this position? Why wouldn't you potentially offer me a position?"*

Then respond to specific concerns in a positive way with a smile on your face (not defensively) with a specific story or two addressing this or that particular concern—not simply saying you are good at this or that. If you are aware of the weakness pointed out, say you have heard that before and are working on it. Ask if the person has any suggestions to help you address that weakness.

# Demonstrate your social skills.

If interviewing on site with several folks from the company:

* ❖ *Walk up to each person and introduce yourself.* Show your social skills and self-confidence;
* ❖ *If you are being informally interviewed along with a group of your friends in a social setting, do not hang with your friends.* Your friends are a crutch in this case and sticking close to them broadcasts to any interviewer your immaturity and a certain lack of self-confidence. Go out on your own and meet your hosts.
* ❖ *Catch and remember the name of each person you meet.* Get a business card if possible or at least write down each person's name and position during the interview;
* ❖ *Get and keep the conversation going* by asking questions of the other person or persons in the conversation. Contribute, but don't dominate.
* ❖ *Make a note about something in particular about each person interviewing you*—something you can mention in your brief follow-up email. Exit the room or go into a corner and jot something down on the back of the business card of each interviewer.

## Prepare for group interviews.

If you get to an on-site group interview situation and/or team activities with other candidates—e.g., group case studies or just a social get-together,

- ❖ **Network actively.** Introduce yourself to everyone you can, including other candidates. If you have a business card (which we suggest, even if you're a student), hand it our liberally, asking for a card or a name in return. Write down the names for those who don't have card.
- ❖ **Speak up and be known.** Do not be a wallflower.
- ❖ **That said, don't dominate conversation.** Don't be that guy/gal whom the group learns to immediately dislike because you don't let anyone else talk.
- ❖ **Let loose a little bit in informal meetings.** Hold non-business conversations at cocktail or other receptions. Walk around and introduce yourself to company personnel. Do not get drunk, but don't be afraid to have a drink or two to loosen up and show your personality.

## Follow up with each employee you met.

Ask for business cards or clearly write down names so you can follow up.

- ❖ Write down names, email addresses, and a few notes on each person and your relevant conversation immediately after your interview.
- ❖ Immediately after the event, send an email **to each person** with whom you spoke. Don't wait—memories (theirs and yours) are short. In your brief email,

  - ❖ Thank the person for spending time with you.
  - ❖ Reference a specific topic or point from your interaction, something she or he can use to remember you—for instance, say, "In our conversation you mentioned..." or, "I was really interested when you talked about..."

- ❖ In your follow-up notes:

  - ❖ **Be succinct,**
  - ❖ **Be enthusiastic, and**
  - ❖ **Do not be presumptuous.** You don't want to pressure anyone—that is, you can mention the opportunity but then simply say something like, "I am enthusiastic about and would very much appreciate being considered for this position." Interviewers value candidates who simply present the facts about themselves and let the interviewers draw their own conclusions regarding the candidates' quality and potential for the position in question. A sure way to get negative vibes is to suggest you are the "ideal candidate" for any position. Your materials and stories must lead the interviewers to conclude on their own that you might indeed be the ideal candidate.

## Demonstrate desirable attitudes.

As reviewed in the previous chapter, the strength and relevance of your resume and supporting materials will play a key role in determining whether or not you move forward through the interview process. But that is not all it will take. Just as important will be **the attitudes you project** in your materials and, especially, in your interviews. Here is a simple reminder list of those attitudes here—refer back to Step 4 for an in-depth explanation of each of these traits.

- ❖ Passion
- ❖ Confidence in uncharted territory
- ❖ Can-do attitude
- ❖ Humble enthusiasm
- ❖ Resilience in turning setbacks into successes
- ❖ Easygoingness

# INTERVIEW DIMENSIONS
# AND SITUATIONS

While prospecting for that first job, you will likely find yourself in a variety of interview situations. These situations can vary dramatically in many ways.

# DIMENSIONS

- ❖ Location—at your school, at a third-party location (e.g., off-campus job fair), or at the target company;
- ❖ Mode—over the phone or face-to-face (in person or via Skype/FaceTime);
- ❖ Length—one to two minutes up to a full day or more;
- ❖ Number of interviewers—one up to a half-dozen or more,
- ❖ Number of back-to-back interviews at the company (potentially five+);
- ❖ Number of interviewees—individual or being grouped with other a number of other candidates;
- ❖ Style—if a group, a case study and presentation with other candidates or a group social situation:
    - ❖ If a case study (with a group of candidates), type and length of case, analysis process, and presentations;[2] and,
    - ❖ If a group social situation, number of candidates and the types and number of company representatives involved.

The specific dimensions that come into play depend upon the particular interview situation. We'll begin with the more typical interview situations for entry-level marketing positions.

# SITUATIONS

## Introductory interviews

- ❖ At a career fair, you might have a face-to-face meeting with one or two company representatives. You will have one to two minutes at most to make a positive impression.
- ❖ As an initial screening, you might speak with someone over the phone, Skype or FaceTime. You might have 5 to 10 minutes (or more) to make an impression. This might happen, for example, if you are studying abroad and applied for a summer internship opportunity.

## First-round interviews

- ❖ Most first-round interviews last 30 to 60 minutes and involve you meeting one to three company representatives.
- ❖ After a successful interview at a career fair, you might get a face-to-face interview, often at the same place as the fair but a half-day or full day later.
- ❖ After making it through an initial screening or very brief interview, your first-round interview could occur over the phone, Skype, or FaceTime.

## Second-round interviews

- ❖ Some occur on-site, and are often face-to-face, back-to-back meetings with several individual interviews over a three to six-hour period. A meeting with several interviewers at once could follow.
- ❖ Others involve a case study with other candidates and a group of interviewers hearing presentations and then debriefing the group of candidates. After the group interviews, some candidates might receive offers.
- ❖ The company might host a social get-together with other candidates and a large number of employees, including superiors for the relevant position.
- ❖ These could happen over the phone, Skype, or FaceTime. You might have several back-to-back sessions with a series of interviewers or one meeting with several representatives at once. These interviews could be spread out over a half-day.

## Additional closing rounds

- ❖ Most final interviews are on-site, face-to-face meetings.
- ❖ One or two people in the organization whom you have not yet met might still want or need to talk with you prior to the company potentially extending you an offer.

# Typical Interview Questions[3]

## INTRODUCTORY QUESTIONS

Prepare and practice answers for general introductory questions on essential topics, such as:

## The job

*"What made you decide to apply for this job?"*

The interviewer wants a considered response that refers specifically to the job description and requirements and then jumps to your academic background, work history, and other experiences that prepare and qualify you for this position. Anyone who stumbles with a candid answer like, "Well, I need a job and this seemed like an interesting possibility," or offers a similar underwhelming response will immediately be dismissed from consideration.

## Your career goals

*"What position and career do think you would like to pursue?"*

Reflect on the deliberations you did in Step 1, when you asked that same question of yourself and (at least tentatively) answered that question. Practice that answer.

## The company

*"What do you know about XYZ Company?"*

This question tests your seriousness and true interest in the position. The interviewer wants to know whether you have you done your homework on the company. If you completed the search process presented in Step 3, you should be fully ready for this question, given your extensive Internet research in searching for, evaluating, and eventually targeting this particular position. Be ready for factual questions such as, who is the CEO? What is the company's business? What products/services do they sell? Who are the target customers? How old is the company? How many employees does it have? What are its sales and sales growth trends?

You should practice describing the company prior to your interview. It is okay to bring a folder that contains copies of your resume, some information about the company, and a copy of the job description, as this reinforces to the recruiter that you have researched the company and position.

## The position

*"What do you know about this particular position?"*
*"What do you anticipate would be your day-to-day role?"*

Have you done your homework not just on the company but also on the position? Be ready for questions about the job description and requirements. Practice describing the position to show the interviewer you fully understand and know what the job entails. Incorporate key words from the published job description and requirements in your resume, cover letters, and your interviews.

## Your qualifications for the position

*"What makes you suitable for this position?"*

This question will probably immediately follow the question, "What do you know about this position?" The interviewer knows you are young and have little traditional work experience. The interviewer wants to see your ability to relate your background and experiences to the job requirements of the position. So, to answer, launch into the leadership stories you specifically developed to evidence your relevant skills, experiences, and strengths. Use key words from the job requirements to tell your stories, showing a natural fit.

## Your readiness for the position

*"What do you hope to learn from this job?"*

This is a roundabout way of finding out a candidate's strengths and weaknesses and the amount of training that would be required prior to this person becoming a productive employee. If a candidate wants to develop a whole new skill set and the company does not have a training program designed for that, this person will not be a good match. On the other hand, if the company has a strong training program and the candidate is clearly bright and highly motivated, he or she could be a good fit. For certain marketing positions, some companies prefer to train bright new employees from scratch—for example, hiring someone with an engineering or mathematics degree for a marketing analytics position.

## About you in general

*"Tell me about yourself."*
*"Walk me through your resume."*

These questions are designed to see if you can articulate the key parts of your resume and background that are most suitable for the position. To answer, very quickly summarize your background, including a fast list of relevant experiences and internships, and then immediately launch into one of your strongest leadership stories developed in Step 2. In that story, integrate key words from the job requirements. Practice giving that answer and telling that story!

# BEHAVIORAL QUESTIONS

*"Tell me about a time when you…"*

If you make it through the first brief interview experience and receive an invitation for further discussions with the company, find out what questions interviewers are likely to ask in these more in-depth interviews. Check out Glassdoor and Quint Careers for hundreds of such questions and sample responses.[4]

Many companies and interviewers ask a series of behavioral questions focusing on your past experiences and often starting with something like, "Tell me about a time you had to deal with…"—some examples appear below. You can't possibly prepare for every potential question, but you might be able to draw on some of your leadership stories. Try to answer some of the questions below, then go online and see some alternative responses.[5] This will help get you used to thinking on your feet and responding to expected and unexpected behavioral questions.

### *Example behavioral questions*[6]

* Give two examples of things you've done in previous jobs or school that demonstrate your willingness to work hard.
* What is the most competitive work or school situation you have experienced? How did you handle it? What was the result?
* Tell me about a time when you built rapport quickly with someone under difficult conditions.
* Some people consider themselves to be "big picture people" and others are detail-oriented. Which are you? Give an example to illustrate this.
* Describe a situation where you felt you did not communicate well. How did you correct the situation?
* Give an example of a time you made poor decision or did something that just didn't turn out right.
* What do you do when you are faced with an obstacle on a project? Given an example or two.
* Tell me about the most difficult or frustrating individual you've ever had to work with, and talk about how you managed to work with that person.
* Describe a time where you positively influenced the actions of others.
* Tell me about a recent job or campus experience that you would describe as a real learning experience. What did you learn?
* Describe a team experience you found disappointing. What could you have done to prevent it?
* Describe a time when you had to make a difficult choice between your personal and professional (or academic) life.
* On occasion we are confronted by dishonesty in the workplace or in school. Tell me about a time you faced this and your response.

If asked about a situation that you cannot remember having faced, then make up a hypothetical situation, starting with, "Well, I do not recall facing that particular situation, but if I did, then..." or, "then I think I would..." This leads quite naturally to the next section on situational questions.

# SITUATIONAL QUESTIONS[7]

*"What would do in a situation when ... happens?"*

Situational questions test how well you can you think on your feet to address any of a series of hypothetical problematic business or personal situations. Such questions typically start with "What would you do if..." or "How would you handle..." As with the behavioral questions, hopefully you can draw on some of your leadership stories to respond to such questions.

These could be somewhat detailed or short, simple questions. For example, "How would you handle an angry customer who was promised delivery of a product on a certain date, but because of manufacturing delays, the company could not deliver on a timely basis? The customer is demanding compensation for the unexpected delay." Another example: "How would you handle a disgruntled employee in your department who has made a habit of arriving late and regularly causes disruptions in everyday office work patterns and expectations?"

For preparation, develop your own answers for some of the shorter situational questions below. Then go online and review some alternative responses.[8]

*Examples of situational questions*[9]

* What would you do if a subordinate or colleague began performing poorly?
* How would you handle it if you believed strongly in a recommendation you made in a meeting, but most of your coworkers shot it down?
* In a training session, you find that the trainer has a thick accent, and you can't understand what's being said. What would you do?
* What would you do if you realized at deadline time that a report you wrote for your boss or professor was not up to par?
* A coworker tells you in confidence that he plans to call in sick while actually taking a week's vacation. What would you do and why?
* What would you do if you strongly disagreed with the way your supervisor told you to handle a problem?
* How would you attempt to make changes in the process if you felt a policy of your organization was hurting its members/workers?
* What would a good manager do to build team spirit?
* What would you do if two teammates were embroiled in a conflict that kept your overall team from completing its task?
* In a leadership role, you find out a team member went over your head to propose an idea or complain about an issue. How would you handle this?

# CRITICAL THINKING QUESTIONS[10]

❖ *How many Christmas trees are there in California?*
❖ *How much does the Willis Tower weigh?*
❖ *How many piano tuners are there in Atlanta?*

When you get out in the workplace, every day you will experience new challenges you have never faced before. You will not have a textbook to refer to every time you run up against new situations. Will you always have to go ask someone else? Will you always have to look up something? Or are you smart enough and self-confident enough to figure out and resolve new challenges on you own? This doesn't mean that you can never seek help or advice from others or that you cannot consult multiple sources easily found online. It means that you are ready, willing, creative, and self-confident enough to try to sort out and resolve solvable problems on your own—even if you have never faced that particular challenge before and even if you have no data actually on hand.

If you cannot demonstrate your personal willingness, adeptness, creativity, and self-confidence to tackle the new or unexpected in your interviews, then you might not be viewed as ready for prime time and many prospective employers might not take a chance on moving you forward in the interview process.

To exhibit your critical thinking skills, grant yourself permission to come up with a wrong answer. The interviewer doesn't care about the answer. These questions see if and how well you can think through a new problem. They test your skills at organization, thoroughness, creativity, approximation, and willingness to provide the wrong answer—because for such questions there is seldom a right answer.

Constant innovation is key to long-term growth. Most innovations are destined for failure. Yet, without constant innovation, few companies can thrive over time. Companies want creative, organized, critical thinkers who are not afraid to venture into the unknown and make mistakes. These questions test that entire set of characteristics. If an interviewer asks you such a question, she or he wants to see your thought process, your ability to identify the pieces of the problem and make a reasonable assumption on each without looking something up, and your method in putting it all together to come up with an answer.

There are four common responses to such questions or problems—
❖ I don't know. Wrong!
❖ Let me see if I can look that up somewhere. Wrong!
❖ Ask for more information. For example, "By 'weight of the Empire State Building,' do you mean with or without furniture? Do I count the people in it?" Wrong—but getting closer! Questions like this are a distraction and just postpone starting to solve the problem.
❖ Approximate the answer. Right! Approximating starts with partitioning the problem into manageable chunks, systematically making a series of educated guesses without actual data (using your general knowledge and common

sense to fill in the blanks), then putting it all together to come up with a number.

*Are you ready for this? Try it. How many Christmas trees are in California?*

What are the questions you would ask to determine that? Estimate the answer to each. Now put together all those approximations into your educated guess about the number of Christmas trees in California.

If you expect us to tell you the answer and are not willing to try that yourself, you missed the point. Go ahead and try it. There is no right answer—only opportunities to exercise ingenuity in identifying the pieces, making reasonable approximations, and linking the pieces of the puzzle into an estimate. Chances are, you will come up with a pretty realistic number. Letting that freedom of thought become a normal and habitual part of your thinking will make you a better critical thinker and a better problem solver.

# OFF-THE-WALL, ODDBALL QUESTIONS

*"If you were a superhero, what would you want your superpowers to be?"*
*"If you had only six months left to live, what would you do with the time?"*

These are wild card, seemingly oddball questions that seem to have nothing to do with anything related to the job for which you are interviewing. They test:

* ❖ Are you willing and able to think on your feet?
* ❖ Can you come up with an original, non-preprogrammed answer?
* ❖ How creative are you?
* ❖ Do you have a sense of humor?
* ❖ How do you handle stress? Do you easily get rattled?

The key to responding to any off-the-wall question is not to let it rattle you. There is no wrong answer to these questions. Smile, take a deep breath, and take a moment to think before you respond. You don't have to brilliant or witty. Be yourself and give an honest response. If you simply cannot think of an answer, ask to come back to that question later. You may lose a few thinking-on-your-feet points but you'll gain points for handling a difficult situation with poise. See some examples below to give you the flavor for such questions. Studying that list will not help, since these specific questions probably won't be asked, but trying to answer a few questions will help you practice answering the unexpected, so you are less likely to be surprised and rattled by such questions.[11]

*Examples of off-the-wall questions*

* ❖ If someone wrote a biography about you, what would the title be?
* ❖ If you could eat dinner with anyone from history, who would it be? Why?
* ❖ If you won $20 million in the lottery, what would you do with the money?
* ❖ Who do you admire the most and why?

- ❖ In a news story about your life, what would the headline say?
- ❖ List three positive character traits you DON'T have.
- ❖ If you were a *Star Wars* character, which one would you be?
- ❖ If you could trade places with any other person for a week, famous or not, living or dead, real or fictional, with whom would you trade?

# SAMPLE INTERVIEW QUESTIONS

Check out the interview section of Glassdoor to find questions you might face in interviews for a specific position at a specific company. Glassdoor includes an interview section for most major companies. The content is particularly insightful since it comes directly from that company's employees. For example, consider the Glassdoor interview section for Nielsen:

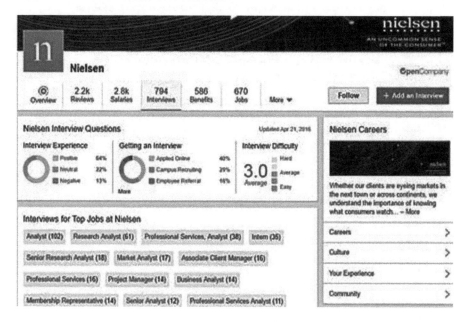

As described earlier, Glassdoor includes an extensive section of sample entry-level marketing interview questions and responses drawn from interview reports from employees of thousands of different companies in general or arranged by city. For example:

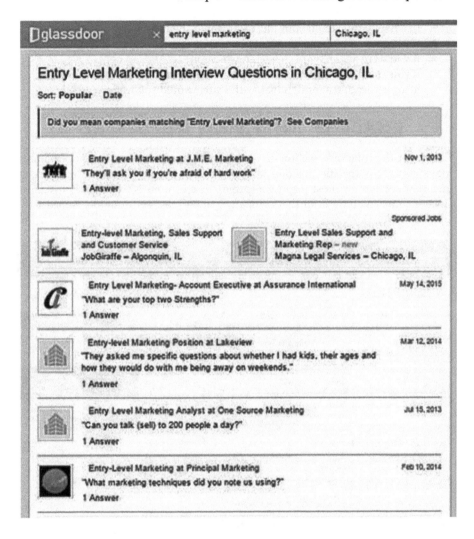

# UNIQUE DEMANDS OF A SALES INTERVIEW

Most people who start in sales actually want a long-term career in sales. As considered in Step 1, however, others starting in sales might realize that many companies require a stint in sales (i.e., you must pay your dues) before eventually moving on to positions as marketing, product or brand managers.[12]

Regardless of the motivation, anyone hoping to interview successfully for a sales position must evidence a rather uniquely demanding set of professional and personal characteristics. These include:

- A willingness and ability to quickly and continuously learn about and keep up with the dynamic list of products or services being sold as well as with ever-changing customer demands and competitive forces;
- Discipline and maturity, because you will very often be on your own to make things happen;
- Evidence of being a self-starter, organized and disciplined enough to make a sales call schedule and stick to it, day after day and month after month;
- A competitive drive to win because sales compensation typically includes a significant commission component as well as sizeable bonuses for meeting challenging quotas;
- Resilience—you will hear 'no' more often than 'yes'.
- Perhaps most importantly, natural communication and social skills—an upbeat, easygoing personality and a readiness not only to meet new people but to enthusiastically and empathetically engage with them.
- Finally, honesty and integrity, attending to one's promises once given and committing to a selling philosophy of under-promising and over-delivering, rather than vice-versa.

If you are interviewing for a sales position, be prepared to evidence to your interviewers that you are aware of and possess each of these must-have traits. Use them as key words and phrases in your resume and cover letters. Develop specific leadership stories that focus on and demonstrate them. Your story titles should include these same key words and phrases. Practice telling these stories to family, friends, colleagues, and career counselors.

# AFTER YOUR FIRST-STAGE INTERVIEW

## POINTS TO CONSIDER

Here we identify series of *points to mention and clearly communicate* when you have been called in for a follow-up interview—that is, when the company is obviously interested in you. Bringing up these topics makes your interest in the position obvious to your interviewers. Discussing each of these points also clearly projects your desire to do whatever is necessary and/or beneficial to enhance the probability of this entry-level job turning into a long-term career.

These points can really differentiate you, as they suggest a level of interest and personal maturity that others interviewing for the same position may not have. Know and bring up these topics or issues as the occasion dictates. Practice the different pieces so you are both clear and comfortable with expressing as many of these points as feasible during your later stage interviews.

- *Career.* You are interested in a career, not a job
- *Rotational Opportunities.* The more exposure to different areas of the company, the better—preferably an opportunity early on in your career to

rotate through several potential functional areas—so you can find one or more areas where you think you can be of most value to the company and so you can learn what areas you can grow into as your career progresses and you gain more experience.

❖ **Willingness to go anywhere and take any job where you can be of most value to the company.** You are willing to work anywhere and to work whatever hours are required to provide maximum value for company. If you are successful with most companies, in a couple years you will most likely be able to move to a preferred location. If you insist on a specific location and then interview only for jobs in that location, realize that you may have just cut out 50-60-70 percent or more of your opportunities.

❖ **Desire to be an integral part of and grow over time with a dynamic, fast-paced, forward-looking company.** You know that if the company is successfully growing, you will have a better chance of contributing and starting to craft a successful career for yourself.

❖ **Readiness for responsibility, love of new challenges, confidence to make mistakes.** You are not afraid of unknown waters, and you hope for and look forward to facing new challenges every day. You realize that facing new challenges will enable you to learn more each day and in doing so become more valuable to the company. As part of this, you are prepared to admit to and learn from your mistakes.

❖ **Mentor.** You hope for a committed mentor, someone who:
  ❖ Is genuinely interested in your career;
  ❖ Will watch your back and guide you constructively when you make mistakes early on;
  ❖ Will provide regular advice on what skills to work on; and,
  ❖ Will alert you when appropriate new opportunities open up— opportunities that would further broaden your experience and your value to the company.

# YOUR POST INTERVIEW FOLLOW-UP[13]

You can go from being the No. 1 priority candidate to the last just by failing to follow up with those who interviewed you. Inversely, a thoughtful follow-up note can readily move you ahead of other candidates.

## Why?

On the positive side, a quick, well-thought out follow-up note:

❖ First and foremost, shows good manners while reinforcing your interest in the position and simultaneously keeping you on the recruiter's front page;
❖ Provides an opportunity to expand, reinforce, or clarify anything in your resume or other relevant interesting topic that came up in your interview;
❖ Shows your persistence at pursuing a potential opportunity, as persistence reflects habits and skills that will be needed in most marketing jobs.

On the negative side, failure to immediately follow-up:

❖ May immediately eliminate you from the mix, as the recruiter will interpret your lack of immediate follow-up as a lack of manners, common sense, discipline, and, most importantly, interest in the position;

❖ Moves those who did follow-up immediately ahead of you in competition.

## When and to whom?

❖ Send an email within 24 hours while it's still fresh on the recruiter's mind (as well as yours), and

❖ Send a separate note to each individual person you met with.

## What to include?

❖ *A header* (even in an email). In the header, include the person's name, the person's title and the company name. You can find each person's title on the business card you should have requested, from earlier communications, or from LinkedIn.

❖ *Thanks*. First, always, thank them for the opportunity to meet and for taking time out of their day to do so.

❖ *Three proven differentiators*. Next, indicate (in bullet points) three items (from your resume, leadership stories told, and general discussion) that evidence your qualifications as a solid fit for the prospective position. These should line up with the main job requirements and, wherever possible, should include some numerical or percentage improvements for which you were responsible.

❖ *No presumptions.* Do not suggest that you are the right candidate for the role. Let the reader self-conclude that from the evidence you provide.

❖ *Emphasize your interest.* Finally, close by again expressing your strong interest in the position and indicating that you will follow-up with them again within a specified time frame. Near the end of the interview itself, you should have asked about the next step and for the decision time frame for that next step. Use the decision time frame the interviewer gave you at a guideline.

❖ *Thank them, again*, for their time and consideration.

❖ *Cordial close.*

## Second follow-up note

Send a second follow-up note no more than five working days after the first one, following this structure:

❖ Begin with a pleasantry, followed by a sentence explaining where you left off during your last communication. "You had indicated that on approximately (*day of the week*) you would be selecting those who would continue the interview process, and I wanted to express my continued interest in being considered for the position."

❖ Include something of value in your follow-up, instead of nagging. Perhaps you have been honing a skill required for the position (mention how you are doing that—maybe starting an online course or reading several books), continuing to work on a project referred to earlier in your three key points (spell out the progress you are continuing to make), or volunteering (e.g., if unemployed) doing something specific that speaks to one or more of the most important job requirements.

❖ Finally, indicate the next follow-up you will initiate. Don't ask them to call you back. Instead, let them know that "I'll follow up again in a few days, but in case you need to reach me, here is the best contact number: XXX-XXX-XXXX."

❖ Cordial close.

# ADDITIONAL POST-INTERVIEW TIPS

Here are some additional post-interview tips from career coach Dana Manciagli.[14]

## Don't:

❖ *Group thank you notes* (one email to two or more people). These imply you are lazy. By their very nature, group notes are not personal!

❖ *Misspellings, grammar, punctuation errors.* Your communication is a writing sample for the employer. Spell-check and grammar-check, then re-read everything again before sending.

❖ *Gimmicks.* Do not send flowers, a gift, etc. Send nothing.

❖ *Impatience.* Do not be impatient. If the hiring manager gave you a specific date or time frame, it is okay to contact at or near the end of that time frame, but do not press it if you don't receive an immediate response.

## Do:

❖ *Match the communication medium the interviewer has been using* (i.e., returning emails with emails, phone calls with phone calls).

❖ *Leave a voicemail message* (we realize that seems to contradict the point immediately above). If calling and leaving a voicemail, be gracious, positive, and interested. Speak in a respectful manner— for example, "I know you are very busy, but I wanted to follow up on the email I sent you, and I'm still very interested in the position."

❖ *Re-attach all prior emails and previous attachments if following up an email with another email.* Make it easier for the recruiter. When following up with an email, always attach the prior email thread to which you are referring so you can keep the context of the communication. If there was an attachment to the prior email, reattach it, as appropriate. Reattach your original application or cover letter and resume, too, if appropriate.

## Unacceptable excuses for failing to follow up

- ❖ *I'm a shoe-in.* "I knocked the interview out of the park, so no need to send anything since I'll get the job." Well, aside from you being too cocky, which could also have hurt you during the interview itself, the next candidate did send a compelling note and is still in the running. You are not because of your impoliteness in not sending an immediate follow-up.
- ❖ *I don't have their email address.* Lesson learned. Ask for all email addresses while you are interviewing. Check the person's e-mail contact info on LinkedIn if you are linked in with that person. Ask to be connected with that person on LinkedIn. As a last resort, contact the recruiter, HR manager, or anybody else who might be able to provide the relevant e-mail address. Simply say, "I would like to send them a thank you note," so your intention is clear.
- ❖ *Thank you notes seem so phony. I'm not the thank you note type.* First, they should be sincere. Sheer appreciation for their time and for considering you as a candidate should be reason enough to take five minutes to review your notes from that meeting and write a thank you note. Second, if you are not the "thank you note type," then learn to be one now if you expect to get and hold any position.
- ❖ *They told me already that I did not make the cut to the next stage.* You want to add your interviewers to your network and you might want to contact them again sometime in the future. In addition, what if another position opens up? Take the high road and always, always send a thank you note and stay in touch after that. In a thank you note, it is acceptable to add, "If another position opens up within your organization, I would definitely be interested and would very much appreciate your consideration."

# FINAL INTERVIEW STAGE

# WHEN THE OFFER IS FORTHCOMING

## Surprise deal breakers

Before the time comes for your would-be final interviews for any prospective entry-level position, you should have already completed your research on the prospective offer. Your research should have included talking with employees who recently accepted the same position, reading Glassdoor and similar employee reviews, and researching the specific position on the Internet in general. Reflecting the results of that research, you should know full well, prior to getting the actual offer, whether or not you will accept the position, if offered.

In this age of openness and Internet access to all sorts of information on nearly any position offered by any company, there is little excuse for being blind-sided with an offer that contains negative surprises. A negative surprise is anything that might be a deal breaker for you. Just as examples, your personal list of deal breakers might include offer components such as a required internship trial period, a non-competitive salary, an unattractive initial location, or required frequent relocation.

## Handling would-be deal breakers

What if, during your initial interviews, you find a deal breaker about the prospective would-be final offer? Let's say you have found what sounds like a very attractive position in terms of the company, the day-to-day work, your prospective colleagues and new network, etc. But then, in the course of your initial interviews for the position, you discover any prospective offer will almost certainly include a required internship trial period, a non-competitive salary or compensation package, an unattractive initial location, required frequent relocation, and/or any other factor that is an absolute deal breaker for you personally?

Do not automatically dismiss the opportunity. First of all, ask about and confirm whether the relevant deal breaker is fixed or flexible. If supposedly fixed, try to negotiate around it. Use a strategy like this:

 ❖ Say something like, "If that is so, then I am sorry, but I no longer interested in continuing my interviews for the position."
 ❖ If the company is still not flexible, then drop this job option from consideration. Immediately, communicate your decision to each person with whom you have interviewed.
 ❖ If one or more of the powerful folks with whom you interviewed is really impressed by you and your credentials and would really like you to join the team, then your broad communication to multiple parties (including that person) might trigger a more flexible stance.
 ❖ If not, then move on. You lose nothing by asking. There are plenty of other attractive entry-level positions without the relevant deal breaker(s).

## Should you continue to consider positions that are unattractive or otherwise unacceptable?

Before getting the actual would-be offer, you should have talked with employees who recently started working in this position with that company. You should have read multiple Glassdoor reviews and similar employee input. You should have researched the specific position on the Internet. Reflecting the results of that research, you should know, prior to entering any would-be final interview stage, whether or not you would accept the position if offered.

If you decide you do not want and/or that you would not accept an offer for a particular position and company, then drop that option from consideration. Why? Let's say you get the offer. Now you have created several dilemmas for yourself. Should you take it? No, you don't want it. But what if you *don't* get an offer that you do like and do want? What if you *do* get an offer that you do like and want? What if this offer that you don't want pays more or is in a more attractive location than the offer you do want? Now what? Avoid these dilemmas by focusing on attractive prospective positions.

You will not find an entry-level job that is absolutely perfect. But dozens upon dozens are available that will be not only acceptable but also attractive for you as career starters. None will be broadcast to you or handed to you on a platter. Do your research. Explore to find them and then energetically and creatively pursue them.

The interviewing process is certainly challenging for most candidates. With proper preparation and practice, however, you can master your interviews and become a priority candidate for the jobs you want most!

## Step #5 REVIEW QUESTIONS
❖
1. What is the best way to get over the nervousness that comes with anticipating an interview?
2. How long do you have to make your first impression in an initial interview?
3. True or false: You should never say "I don't know" during an interview. Why, why not?
4. What are the different stages of interviewing for a position? How should your interviewing plan and strategy differ for these different stages?
5. True or false: In an interview, it is okay for you to bring along a folder with copies of your resume, information about the company, and a copy of the job description? Why or why not?
6. What is meant by 'behavioral interview questions' and how can you prepare for them?
7. When asked a 'critical thinking interview question,' avoid responding in what ways? How should you respond if you do not know the answer off the top of your head?
8. What are some good resources for finding and practicing sample interview questions?
9. Why is it MANDATORY to always follow up with those who interviewed you? How and when should you follow up?
10. Assume you have made it to the second interview stage or later and now decide you no longer want to pursue a particular job alternative. Specifically, what should you do next? Give your reasoning.

---

1 Draws from collegerecruiter.com/blog/2014/05/22/graduate-tips-deal-interview-nervousness/ and smartrecruiters.com/blog/the-5-be-all-end-all-interview-questions-for-entry-level-jobs/. Also, see The Quintessential Guide to Job Interview Preparation, Hansen, K and R. Hansen, Ph.D. (Quintessential Careers Press), A free book that covers essential information on job interviewing. This comprehensive guide describes what to expect in the various stages of your overall interview process with any company.

2 For discussion, guidelines, tips and examples of interview-related group case analyses and presentations, see amazon.com/Case-Point-Complete-Interview-Preparation/dp/0971015880/ref=sr_1_1?ie=UTF8&qid=1461546224&sr=8-1&keywords=case+in+point

3 Draws from collegerecruiter.com/blog/2014/05/22/graduate-tips-deal-interview-nervousness/ and smartrecruiters.com/blog/the-5-be-all-end-all-interview-questions-for-entry-level-jobs/ Also, see The Quintessential Guide to Job Interview Preparation, Hansen, K and R. Hansen, Ph.D. (Quintessential Careers Press). A free book that covers essential information on job interviewing. This comprehensive guide describes what to expect in the various stages of your overall interview process with any company.

4 glassdoor.com/Interview/entry-level-marketing-interview-questions-SRCH_KO0,21.htm; quintcareers.com/interview-question-database/

5 quintcareers.com/interview-question-database/; quintcareers.com/interview-question-database/college-behavioral-intermediate/

6 Ibid.

7 quintcareers.com/interview-question-database/situational/

8 quintcareers.com/interview-question-database/situational/

9 Ibid.

10 Important input here is from THE ORGANIZED MIND: Thinking Straight in the Age of Information Overload. Copyright © 2014 by Daniel Levitin and wired.com/2014/08/how-to-solve-crazy-open-ended-google-interview-questions/

11 quintcareers.com/interview-question-database/off-the-wall-questions/

12 Refer to earlier discussion of selling and sales careers back in Step 1.

13 This section draws heavily from linkedin.com/pulse/post-job-interview-follow-up-follow-through-part-1-2-dana-manciagli, and linkedin.com/pulse/post-job-interview-follow-up-follow-through-part-2-dana-manciagli, and is complemented by suggestions from recruiters from multiple companies.

14 linkedin.com/pulse/post-job-interview-follow-up-follow-through-part-2-dana-manciagli

# STEP 6
# EVALUATING AND POTENTIALLY NEGOTIATING YOUR OFFER

## QUICK START

You've received an offer. If the offer is for a dream entry-level marketing position that you have actively pursued, you should be elated! Now what do you do?

## Should you accept the offer?

Offers come in all different shapes and sizes. Negotiating an offer might not be necessary if it is for an attractive position that is about as close to your dream job as can be. Regardless, you should always get the offer in writing and take whatever time is necessary to carefully evaluate the offer and to make sure that the position is truly what you want. Accepting an offer should not be a snap decision.

## How should you evaluate your offer?
## What should be in your offer?

More than just the offer, you should analyze how you feel about the industry, company, and the position. If you feel confident about and pleased with all these aspects, then you should review the actual offer. Factors to consider include:

- ❖ Salary
- ❖ Start date
- ❖ Location
- ❖ Bonuses
- ❖ Employee benefits packages
- ❖ Area or division of the company
- ❖ Time off

You can ask about many other topics as well. Some of these include:

- ❖ Expected hours of work

- ❖ Training courses
- ❖ Rotational programs
- ❖ Stock options
- ❖ Promotional opportunities

If you are sure the offer is what you want and you have sufficiently evaluated it, then accepting is a no brainer! That said, other offers might be on the horizon, complicating your decision.

# What if you have another potential offer?[1]

If you are still waiting on a more favored potential offer from Company A, making a decision on an existing offer from Company B be stressful and difficult. The best way to handle this is by reaching out to Company A inquiring about where you stand in their interviewing process and updating them on your current situation with Company B. If you get positive feedback from Company A and believe an offer is on the way, the next step is to contact Company B and ask for an extension on the decision deadline for their offer. If they don't give it to you, there's no harm in waiting until the deadline to make a decision.

# Should you try to negotiate?

In general, entry-level employees don't have as much room to negotiate as do more experienced employees. If you do want to attempt to negotiate your entry-level salary, then the most important thing to know is your worth. Along with asking others at the company about typical starting salaries, many sites online will give you a good estimate of how much you should be offered. If you end up receiving a salary offer that your research shows is lower than what you expected, inquire about increasing it to your well-researched number.

While an entry-level starting salary that is in line with industry standards is typically difficult to negotiate, some other factors may be more negotiable. These include potential adjustments such as the following.

## Monetary adjustments:

- ❖ Signing bonus
- ❖ Relocation bonus
- ❖ Cost of living salary adjustments
- ❖ Bonuses, stock options, or shares
- ❖ Travel expenses/card
- ❖ Parking fees
- ❖ Equipment (e.g., cell phone, laptop)
- ❖ Tuition assistance for continuing studies

## Non-monetary adjustments:

- ❖ Start date
- ❖ Location

- Choice of mentor
- Area or division of the company in which you would prefer to work
- Vacation timing (number of days would be very difficult to negotiate)
- Professional development programs and other educational opportunities
- Enhanced flex time (nonstandard hours) and/or flexible out-of-office work.

## Can you renege on an offer you have accepted?

Reneging on an offer, or rejecting the offer after you have already accepted it, can be done, but the strong counsel is to never renege. Doing so will be a matter of record and can preclude you from ever again receiving a job offer from that same company. Furthermore, recruiters and hiring managers talk to each other. By reneging, you may be tainting your reputation in the field—affecting your opportunities down the line.

## What if a company reneges on your offer?

There are two main reasons a company would renege on an offer made to you:

- For whatever reason, be it a failed drug test, background check, false documentation in your resume, or an inability to maintain your GPA, a check of your background reveals something violating a stated contingency in your contract offer. This is your problem and you have no recourse.
- A company change has affected your offer. This could be anything from new financial constraints to a company merger to changes stemming from a restructuring of the firm. In any case, hopefully the company will only make minor adjustments to your job offer. In the worst-case scenario, however, the company might have to pull the offer. This is not a reflection on you. The best way to handle the situation is to do so as gracefully and maturely as possible.

A company reneging on an offer is not common, but it can happen. The important task is determining why the offer has been taken off the table in order to learn from it as you move forward.

In Step #6, we provide perspectives and suggestions about each of these issues.

# YOU RECEIVE AN OFFER

Let's assume you carefully reviewed the various possible entry-level marketing positions overviewed in Step 1. Let's also assume you came to a well-considered conclusion about the type of position, company culture, location, and the general conditions of employment that most appeal to you. We have been referring to this as your "dream entry-level position."

Now let's also assume you have just received an offer for a position that matches your dream. It is an attractive position that will launch your career with reasonable compensation and with satisfactory or more than satisfactory general conditions of employment.

Should you accept the offer? Even if the offer matches your dream as in the case hypothesized above, you should consider a number of factors in deciding whether or not to accept the offer. This is true even if you are leaning strongly toward immediately taking the offer and are quite certain that you will indeed ultimately accept the position. The factors to consider include:

- ❖ Is it a verbal or written offer?
- ❖ Do you know all the details of the offer?
- ❖ Are you waiting for a potentially more attractive offer from another company?
- ❖ Within the details, are there any 'deal-breakers' that may the job and the offer much less attractive than you originally thought?
- ❖ Might it be possible to negotiate for enhancements in certain monetary or non-monetary components of the position and offer?

Below we consider these and other variables.

# WHAT IF IT'S JUST A VERBAL OFFER?[2]

If you receive only a verbal offer, regardless of how attractive, you are *ALWAYS* better off to avoid making a hard commitment until you have a written version of that offer in hand. With some verbal offers, the employer is trying to close the deal before giving you a chance to potentially negotiate a better salary or other more attractive conditions of employment. So, always get and carefully review a written offer prior to accepting any verbal offer.

For example, upon receiving only a verbal offer, you might immediately respond:

"Thank you so much. I am very pleased with this offer, and I would love to work for XYZ. I am confident that it would be a great career starter for me and that I could do well and contribute significantly to XYZ. Please email me the offer with the associated benefits information and conditions of employment and give me a chance to carefully review it. I will then get back to you in a day or two with what I am certain will be an enthusiastic, positive response. Again, thank you very much for the offer and for your confidence in me and my qualifications."

# CAREFULLY REVIEW THE DETAILS OF THE OFFER

Once you receive the **written offer** for your would-be dream entry-level position, do not immediately accept the offer. You need to carefully study the offer. Accepting an offer prematurely can have negative consequences for years to come.

For example, if you accept a lower salary than is appropriate for the position, this number will also adversely affect the absolute size of your projected raises in the future, which are typically calculated as a percentage of your current salary. If you decide to move to a different company, that company will want to see your salary history and will typically base their offer at least partially upon that history. So, even if you are absolutely delighted to get an offer for a dream position with a great company, take the time to clear your head and consider the offer away from the pressure of an interview or phone conversation.

- ❖ *Pause and step back.* Thank the interviewer or hiring manager and express your delight with the offer, but make sure you have a written version of the offer (see above) and ask for a day or two to consider all the details. This is both reasonable and expected.
- ❖ *Review (or get) all the facts.* Compare the breadth and depth of content in the offer. We review expected offer contents later.
- ❖ *Consult with your trusted advisors* (spouse, significant other, parents, mentors, and/or other confidants) regarding the position and the offer. Consider their input and advice, as they will help you to be more objective in evaluating the position and the various components of the specific offer. Objectivity is paramount because once you sign, you are committed to the position and to the specific terms of the offer.

# A TYPICAL OFFER

Sample Offer Letter
Lincoln Park Financial

May 17, 20xx
Amy Little
207 S. Touhy Ave, Chicago, IL 60601

Dear Ms. Little,

On behalf of Lincoln Park Financial, I am pleased to offer you a position with our company as a full-time employee in the role of a Regional Financial Consultant. This offer is contingent upon the following terms and conditions:

Employment Dates: You will start as a full-time employee of Lincoln Park Financial Corp. effective June 1, 20xx. Your employment with LPF is subject to Illinois' "employment at will" doctrine and this letter is not a contract for employment of any specific duration. Both you and the company have the right to terminate your employment at any time with or without cause.

Position: We are hiring you as a Regional Consultant. This is a full-time, exempt position that reports directly to Jerome Milford, Manager of Regional Consultants. Exempt means that we (LPF) do not have to track your hours or pay them, no matter how many hours you work.

Compensation: You will receive an annual base salary of $50,000 paid out semi-monthly in 24 equal installments. You will also receive a $5,000 bonus paid upon your obtaining a Series 6 Securities license and Illinois Life Insurance license. LPF will cover all costs for these licenses in your first year of employment. After, you will be eligible for quarterly bonuses based on performance. You will also be eligible for an annual bonus based on individual and company performance.

Employee Benefits: Lincoln Park Financial provides our employees with a package of benefits that include: paid vacation; health, dental, vision, and life insurance; flexible spending accounts; health savings accounts; disability insurance; and a 401(k) program. A more thorough description of our employee benefits package is available in the Lincoln Park Employee Handbook. You will receive a copy of the handbook during your new hire orientation.

Background Screen: This offer is contingent upon the successful completion of a background screen. If you do not pass, this offer of employment will be rescinded. This letter represents the complete understanding between you and Lincoln Park Financial regarding the employment relationship and supersedes all prior oral and written communication on that subject. This offer is also contingent upon the successful completion of the attached LPF Application for Employment and Consumer Credit Report Notice and Authorization

Lincoln Park Financial is pleased to extend this official offer. If you choose to accept, please sign in the appropriate space below and return this letter to our corporate office. By signing below, you acknowledge that you have read, understand, and accept the terms of this offer. Should you have any questions, please don't hesitate to contact our HR department at (555) 272-9284.

Thank you and welcome to the Lincoln Park Financial Team!

Sincerely,

Ann Reynolds
Director, Human Resources

Read and Accepted:

Your Signature
Date

# EVALUATING AN OFFER

Is the offer from Lincoln Park Financial a good, acceptable offer for Amy? Should Amy sign and accept it or not? That depends on several factors. First of all, we need to consider the context. Here are the facts.

❖ This position consists primarily of cold calling a lead list of financial advisors to offer some unique LPF tax deferred annuity instruments that the advisors themselves can, in turn, offer and sell to their own clients.

❖ Amy was contacted by phone about this position just last week.

❖ Immediately following the phone interview, she was invited into LPF's Chicago office for a day of interviewing.

❖ She had her interviews on Tuesday of this week and was offered the position the very next day (Wednesday) in a phone call from her would-be immediate superior, Jerome Milford.

❖ That was followed up with the emailed offer letter above from LPF HR Director, Ann Reynolds.

❖ In his phone call, Jerome gave Amy a very short deadline of this Friday to accept or reject the offer.

Let's consider what Amy should do. We start by considering Amy's general attitude regarding the prospective position.

## What does Amy think of the industry, company, position, and offer?

*Scenario #1*: Assume Amy **eschews the financial industry and/or the position** (e.g., the very notion of spending a year or two primarily cold calling) and that the day of on-site interviewing did not change her mind.

*Scenario #2:* Assume Amy targeted a cold calling position such as this in the financial industry and **now sees this specific opportunity as a dream entry-level position**. Let's also assume the offer letter contains *no deal breakers* for her, such as too low a base salary, or what Amy would have regarded as a very unattractive location, or starting date, or whatever.

*Scenario #3:* Assume Amy did not target such a position but was curious about the position and, after the interview, **thinks she might be interested**. However, she does not want to start earlier than August 15, 20XX, which conflicts with the June 1 date in the written offer.

## What should Amy do next?

*In Scenario #1,* Amy should immediately reject the offer with an appropriate phone call and email. In this instance, we can legitimately wonder why Amy even interviewed for this position in the first place.

*In Scenario #2,* after requesting (and in all likelihood receiving) a minimum three-day extension to receive and consider additional information about the specific contents of the employee handbook and to have an opportunity to talk with at least two current employees holding the same position (see specifics below), Amy should and will likely accept the position.

*In Scenario #3,* given that she is not in love with this prospective position, Amy regards the June 1 start date as a deal breaker for her. She should still consider the offer, seek an extension to gather more information (as in Scenario #2 above), and try to get the June start day moved back to August 15 or later.

## Detailed plan for Amy in Scenario #2

This is the scenario in which the position and conditions of employment line up with Amy's dream entry-level position. In this instance, Amy should:

- ❖ Express delight, indicating that in all likelihood she will accept; but
- ❖ Indicate that she needs more information and more time to consider the offer, asking for minimum three-day extension to:
  - ❖ Request, study, and then ask questions about anything unclear in the employee handbook; and then
  - ❖ After studying the handbook, talk with at least two people currently working in her prospective position—asking them specific questions such as the following.

### Ask specific questions about the offer letter.

- ❖ *Hours of work expected:* Given the specified "exempt status" of the offer (no overtime pay), how many hours do you work in a typical week?
- ❖ *Bonuses:* How often have you and others in this position made your quarterly and annual bonuses and how much have the bonuses been? Bottom line, how much did you make in year one? Year two?
- ❖ *Quotas:* Does an individual's quota increase every quarter? Every year? If so, how realistic and attainable have your personal increased quotas been?
- ❖ *Licensing course:* Has anyone failed to make it through the licensing course and had to pay back the cost of that training? If so, how much?
- ❖ *Time off:* How many days of vacation did you get and actually use last year? Were you able to take them when you wanted to? Were you expected to report back to work during vacation? How many holidays and sick days did you get and actually use last year?
- ❖ *Flextime and telecommuting*: Are you regularly (or ever) able to work non-traditional hours or work out-of-office?

❖ **Employee benefits package:** Compared with the packages of your friends working at other companies, do you think LPF's employee package is competitive? Have you been disappointed in any aspect(s) of it?

## Ask more general questions about working at LPF

❖ **Work-life balance:** Are folks in this position at LPF generally happy? How is the company culture and work-life balance? Have you met and enjoyed your immediate colleagues—in and out of the workplace environment?

❖ **Promotion opportunities:** How much time does it take the typical employee to get a promotion to the next level? What is the typical next level and how much has the overall annual income increased?

❖ **Superiors and company leadership:** What is your general opinion of your immediate superior and LPF company leadership and support in general? Are there any negatives that turn you off or that concern you?

❖ **Positives:** What's the best part of working in this position and/or for LPF?

❖ **Negatives:** What's the worst or most difficult part of working in this position and/or working for LPF?

❖ **Those who leave LPF:** How many started with you in your class at LPF? How many of those left within year 1? Year 2? Why do you think they left?

❖ **Career at LPF:** How long do you see yourself working at LPF? If you anticipate leaving in 3-5 years or less, why do you think you would likely leave?

Then, if no deal breakers pop up in the handbook review and employee interviews, she should accept the offer with a phone call, followed by an acceptance letter like the one shown earlier.

# Detailed plan for Amy in Scenario #3

This is the scenario in which the position and conditions of employment might work for Amy, if she can get a few things clarified and also get the start date moved back to August 15. In this instance, Amy should act in two phases.

## Phase 1

❖ Indicate that she is pleased with the offer; but

❖ Say that she needs more information and more time to consider the offer, asking for minimum three-day extension to:
   ❖ Request, study, and then ask questions about anything unclear in the employee handbook; and then
   ❖ After studying the handbook, talk with a minimum of two people currently working in her prospective position. Ask them specific questions about the offer letter and general questions on working at LPF (see above).

## Phase 2

If no deal breakers emerge in the employee interviews or in the employee handbook, Amy should:

❖ Call LPF next Tuesday or Wednesday and say she will take the position if she can start on August 15 or after and LPF can make other adjustments to the contract she feels are necessary based on reviewing the handbook and talking with current employees (there might not be any other adjustments desired).

❖ If LPF says "no" to start late (e.g., perhaps they have a training class for all new employees starting June 1) or "no" to modifying any other deal breakers she found in reviewing the LPF Employee Handbook and talking with employees, then this opportunity was simply not meant to be and she should reject it.

❖ If LPF comes through with both the later date and the other deal-breaker changes Amy has requested, then she should accept the offer with a phone call, followed by an acceptance letter like the one shown earlier.

In this scenario, Amy realizes that this position might not be her perfect dream entry-level position, but she also knows she will:

❖ Have a job;
❖ Receive free-of-charge valuable financial advisor training and licensing;
❖ Start her career with a solid company and network: and that
❖ She can move on in as little as a year or two if this does not work out.

# WHAT IF YOU ARE WAITING ON AN OFFER FROM ANOTHER COMPANY?[3]

Consider this rather common scenario for any job seeker. You just received an attractive offer from Company B. You have been given a two-week deadline to accept. Do such deadlines occur? Certainly! The company has others lined up for the position if you reject it. You have also been interviewing with Company A, and you are both hoping for and optimistically expecting an offer. *You favor the would-be offer from Company A.*

You have not heard recently from Company A and fear you might not hear until after Company B's deadline. Although you feel you would prefer Company A, you definitely want a job and you regard the Company B position and offer as generally attractive and more than satisfactory for your first job.

## What do you do?

You know (or will soon learn from discussion near the end of this step) that you will not renege if you officially accept Company B's offer and then later get an offer from Company A. So, what should you do?

*Contact Company A*—the sooner, the better.

❖ Call Company A and let your contact know the situation. Be candid. They have heard this situation before and will be understanding.

❖ Keep your information simple and factual regarding the offer from Company B. You can mention Company B by name if you prefer.

❖ Ask where you stand in the evaluation process and ask: "What are the prospects for me getting a decision from Company A prior to my deadline with Company B?"

❖ Reiterate to Company A that you really want to work for them and would in all likelihood accept an offer from Company A in preference to the existing offer from Company B.

If Company A cannot commit to a decision on you prior to the Company B deadline, then press to know exactly when the decision would be forthcoming. Understand that many advertising agencies in particular are hesitant to make commitments until they know their often very dynamic manpower needs for specific clients.

In sum, these are your goals with Company A:

❖ Learn more about your status;
❖ Re-affirm your interest in the position; and, perhaps,
❖ Stimulate Company A to speed up their decision process on you if they really want you.

Next, after your exchange with Company A, if you still have realistic expectations of an offer ultimately coming from Company A, then immediately **contact Company B**. Express your appreciation to Company B for the offer and indicate that you do not yet have all the information that you need to make your decision.

Like the folks at Company A, your contacts at Company B have heard this situation before and will be understanding. They know that their prime candidates will likely have multiple opportunities. If Company A has agreed to make a decision on you prior to the deadline date, no problem.

## Asking for an Extension

First of all, your chances for Company B extending their deadline are better if you do not wait until the end of the deadline period (e.g., two weeks). That is why it is important to talk to Company A immediately.

If Company A has not agreed to make a decision on you prior to the deadline date, but confirms with you that they will within, say, an additional week or so after your deadline, ask Company B for that specific deadline extension.

If Company A remains uncertain about whether and when it might make an offer to you, you still have the option of asking for a reasonable extension (e.g., an additional week or two), hoping an offer from Company A will be forthcoming.

No extension from Company B means decision time is coming for you at the end of the two-week deadline period. You have nothing to lose by waiting until the deadline date, then accepting or rejecting the offer. Remember, no job, first or last, is perfect. You regard the Company B position and offer as more than satisfactory for your first job. Your first position is all about getting experience. You can get that with Company B. You will do fine at Company B.

Take the offer from Company B. Inform Company A of your choice, while leaving open your line of communications with them for a prospective offer in the future, after you have spent a reasonable time (e.g., 18 months) with Company B.

Your goals with Company B:

- ❖ Maintain your good relationship with Company B; and, if needed,
- ❖ Get Company B to extend its deadline for you.

# NEGOTIATING PRINCIPLES FOR ENTRY-LEVEL CANDIDATES[4]

## General negotiating guidelines

Here is a list of general negotiating principles and guidelines for entry-level candidates.

- ❖ Do not try to negotiate anything during the initial interview process. The time for negotiating, if ever, is only after you receive an offer.
- ❖ Do not try to negotiate anything until you receive and carefully review the offer *in writing*.
- ❖ Negotiation is not a game. Both sides 'win' in a successful negotiation. The candidate would 'win' one or more monetary or non-monetary concessions, enhancing the original offer. The company would win by gaining a well-qualified new employee (plus, perhaps a concession or two from the new employee – see below)
- ❖ Relating again to the notion that 'negotiation is not a game,' do not attempt to negotiate if you would not accept the offer, should you be successful in gaining the offer enhancements desired.
- ❖ Consider the whole package of monetary and non-monetary components in evaluating the overall attractiveness of the offer – before you consider potentially negotiating any particular dimension of the offer.
- ❖ Entry-level candidates have much less negotiating leverage than those with significant experience and those in higher-level positions.
- ❖ **Do** try to negotiate for a higher base salary – **but only if** the salary offer is under what your research shows and what you can clearly verify is typical (the 'industry standard') for this position in the relevant location.
- ❖ If the position is attractive, and you currently feel you would take the offer if it did not include one or two monetary or non-monetary 'deal-breaker(s)' (deal-breakers are discussed elsewhere), then do try to negotiate away the deal breaker(s).
- ❖ Negotiate the whole offer package together. Do not try to negotiate one item, then the next, then the next. Negotiating one item after another may be possible for a more experienced, more seasoned prospective new employee, but is not appropriate for an entry-level candidate.

❖ Prepare a list of your potential 'gives' and your desired 'gets' prior to any negotiation effort. That is, identify components of the written offer that you are willing to give up (something less important to you personally—e.g., perhaps relocation expenses, start date, or even base salary level – depending on your situation) for somethings ('gets') that are very important to you (e.g., location, vacation timing or days, or early performance and salary review). When negotiating, always capture a 'get' before you offer a 'give.' (we provide an example of this.)

❖ Once you accept the offer, you lose any leverage you may have had for negotiating enhancements to that offer.

The discussion below expands upon some of these general principles and guidelines.

# POTENTIALLY NEGOTIATING SALARY

## Know what you are worth.

There is no excuse for being surprised by the salary offered for an entry-level marketing position. In addition to having had the opportunity to ask others in the company during the interview process, you have plenty of resources at your disposal to make you well aware of the salary range for virtually any prospective entry-level marketing position at any company in any location. Here are additional sources for researching salary information:[5]

❖ NACE Salary Calculator (naceweb.org)
❖ Salary.com: Lists salary information by job type and region.
❖ Glassdoor.com: Lists salaries for a variety of positions for many companies.
❖ JobStar.org: Offers links to 300 salary surveys.

## What if you receive a low salary offer?

Entry-level salaries for most positions are seldom negotiable. That said, let's assume your research clearly indicates that the specific annual salary proposed in your otherwise attractive offer is lower than the typical industry standard for this entry-level marketing position and location. You have been low-balled. Do not accept the offer as-is because doing so could easily negatively impact your earnings for years to come, in future raises with this company and in any prospective move to another company. You are worth what the market will pay. What to do?

If the low-ball offer comes via email, immediately reply by e-mail in a professional manner:

> Dear Ms. Albright,
>
> Thank you and ABC Market Research very much for the offer for the position of Assistant Marketing Analyst for the annual salary of $43,000. I

am very pleased to receive this offer and am excited at the prospect of joining your marketing team.

My only reservation concerns the proposed starting salary. My research (NACE, Salary, Glassdoor, and JobStar) on salaries for comparable positions in Chicago shows an average expected salary of approximately $52,000. If you can modify the offer to meet that, I am prepared to accept.

Again, I emphasize that I would love to accept your offer and join your team at ABC. I am hopeful that we can come to an agreement on the starting salary so I can pursue that dream.

Sincerely,
Brian Jordan

If you receive the low-ball offer by phone, express thanks and enthusiasm, but do not indicate you will accept the offer. Ask for a written offer. This gives you a chance to research the expected salary (in case you haven't already done so). Then, when you receive the written offer, reply with the same e-mail note as above.

## You can accept a low salary.

If the salary offered is already in line with industry standard salaries for similar positions in the relevant location, then, unless you have some highly visible, significant experience and qualifications, do not fool yourself into thinking that you can negotiate for a significant increase in entry-level salary. Colleagues can quite easily learn each other's base salaries. With morale a high priority, a company can feel handcuffed by specific starting salary offers already made to and accepted by others for the same position.

If after your research you are still very disappointed with the prospective starting salary, then either resign yourself to that low starting compensation and continue pursuing this position or change directions and pursue an alternative, higher-paying entry-level position. You have to deal with reality.

All is not lost if you accept the low salary that is typical for certain entry-level marketing position. Consider that the first salary raise for many such positions is often very significant (up to 50 percent or more). For example, an entry-level media planner at an advertising agency might make only $35 to $38,000 per year to start, but quickly make $50,000 to $55,000 per year or more after only a year or two of solid performance.

## POTENTIALLY NEGOTIABLE BENEFITS

## Which enhanced benefits might you realistically pursue? Do your homework.

First, clarify the benefits that come with the offer. Most companies have an employee handbook—request and carefully review it.

Next, find out what other entry-level employees of this company have successfully negotiated. Explore this during the interview process in candid conversations with those now in your would-be position. Seek out observations and suggestions from this company's employees (in person) and/or from Glassdoor and other Internet sites.

Again, not much is negotiable for the entry-level employee, but your bargaining power will increase as you gain some experience. Below is a list of benefits you can consider negotiating.

# Negotiable benefits

## Early performance and salary review

If you receive a low-ball offer but you are still strongly attracted to the job, consider asking for an earlier-than-normal performance and salary review. Most employers review performance and salaries yearly. Asking for a nine-month or even six-month review might be a realistic target. As a general principle, do not try to negotiate this if you are satisfied with your salary offer (save whatever negotiating leverage you have for other items).

## Direct monetary adjustments

As an entry level candidate, you can consider negotiating for any of these that are important to you – but only do this if you know that others now in your position at the company or other current candidates for this position received these in their offers.

*   *Signing Bonus:* Ask for one, if not offered, or ask for a higher one if offered – but only commensurate with what other candidates for the same position have been offered.
*   *Relocation bonus:* Ask for one, if not offered, or ask for an increase – especially if you can show that your moving and transition expenses will be significant. As with the other monetary and non-monetary benefit adjustments, your request is more likely to be successful if others in the same position have been granted such a bonus.
*   *Cost of living salary adjustments:* Negotiate if you'll be working in a higher-cost city like New York, San Francisco, Washington D.C., Boston, Los Angeles, or Chicago versus much lower-cost cities such as Louisville, St. Louis, Cleveland, Detroit, Cincinnati, or Shreveport.[6]
*   *Other bonuses:* Ask about stock options and shares—if others in your position received these, you should too.
*   *Travel expenses:* If you're weighing a job offer that requires extensive travel, remember that for these types of professionals, work-travel expenses that range from gas mileage to frequent flier miles and even corporate credit card access are relevant for discussion and negotiation.
*   *Parking fees:* Parking fees can run to $100 per month or more. Find out if others in your position have negotiated some financial help in this area. If so, consider doing so yourself as well.

❖ *Equipment:* Asking for a company cell phone because you're expected to be on call is within reason, but asking for an iPhone with an unlimited data plan could be pushing it, particularly for an entry-level employee. Many companies offer laptops, phones, and tablets for certain employees. If others in your position received these, why not you?

## Non-monetary benefits

❖ *Start date:* It's typically not difficult to negotiate your start date unless a company has targeted you as part of particular incoming class that will start training on a specific date.

❖ *Location:* Consider negotiating your city or location within a particular city (e.g., downtown location or location in the Chicago suburbs) if that is important to you. Making this a personal 'deal-breaker,' however, is not advised, as it will significantly curtail your opportunities in general. Get some experience first. With solid performance under your belt, location becomes much more negotiable with most companies and you can move with the company to your target city within a couple of years.

❖ *More flexible work conditions*: Discuss flex time, telecommuting, non-traditional work schedule and place (e.g., some work at home during normal work hours).

  ❖ Before negotiating in this area (flextime & work location), find out the current employees' feelings about the corporate culture and work-life balance. If employees are highly satisfied with the work environment, negotiating for a more flexible work environment should not be a priority.

  ❖ Asking for a non-traditional work schedule or workspace is no longer that unusual, given employees' rising concern for work-life balance, particularly among those in more stressful day-to-day environments. Even in those situations, negotiating something in this area will be more difficult for new employees unless other new employees in similar positions have also negotiated more flexible working conditions.

❖ *Paid professional development or educational opportunities:* This perk benefits you and the company for both the short and long term. Plus, this request signals to a hiring manager that you're conscientious about doing well and growing professionally. Ask about opportunities the company provides for advancement, certifications, and additional development training. The occasional class fee is different from tuition reimbursement, which is a major perk and very difficult to negotiate if it is not already in the employee handbook and an integral part of corporate policy and commitment.

❖ *Choice of mentor*. This might be particularly important if you interned with the company and you have a particular, preferred mentor in mind. A well-chosen mentor can enhance your career development in many ways.

❖ *Area or division of the company:* Consider with what division or product/service area you would prefer to work. This may or may not be negotiable for an entry-level marketing position, but it can't hurt to ask. If nothing else, asking broadcasts your interest in potentially working with that other division or product/service area, should such an opportunity arise in the future.

❖ *Vacation timing*: The number of days would be very difficult to negotiate for an entry-level employee, but timing of vacation is typically negotiable.

# NEGOTIATING STRATEGY

When negotiating, always remember to 'get' before you 'give'—meaning, for example, do not offer (give) a willingness to work at a generally less desirable location or agree to a 'non-optimal' start date (e.g., June 1, right after you graduate) unless the employer first agrees to meet a highly desirable 'get' such as an early performance and salary review or assignment to a division or product/service area that is particularly attractive to you.

Example: For requesting a *smaller change* in the offer, such as 'Start Date'.'

> *Candidate:* "Is it possible for me to start in August rather than June 1?"
>
> *Employer:* "Not likely, but I could inquire."
>
> *Candidate:* "Well, if I could start August 15 rather than June 15, then I'd be willing to take $1,000 less in relocation expenses."
>
> *Employer:* "Okay, I'm pretty sure we can work that out."
>
> *Candidate*: "Otherwise, we leave the expense package as-is and I start as planned."—The candidate adds that to ensure that the employer doesn't take his give (lower expense package) without guaranteeing the desired get (start in August).

Example. For requesting a *larger change* in the offer, such as your assigned division:

> *Candidate*: "Might it be possible for me to work in the ABC Division, rather than the XYZ Division?
>
> *Employer*: "Not likely, but I could inquire."
>
> *Candidate*: "Well, if we could change so I work in the ABC Division, then I'd be willing to move wherever works best for the company."
>
> *Employer*: "Well, that's showing the kind of initiative and flexibility we are looking for in our new employees. I'll see if we can work that out."
>
> *Candidate*: "Okay, if you can change the offer to put me in the ABC Division, then I'd be willing to move whatever location would work best for the company. Otherwise, I'll start in Minneapolis, as now planned."

# ACCEPTING AND REJECTING

## TO ACCEPT:

Assume that, after due consideration of the detailed written offer, you and your advisors conclude that the specifics of the offer match most of the criteria of your dream entry-level position. After a day of two of deliberation, accept the offer. Do so by sending a brief acceptance letter such as this:

---

Dear Ms. Roberts,

Thank you very much for the offer. I have reviewed the specifics and accept the offer with enthusiasm.

Please consider this email as my formal acceptance of the Assistant Market Analyst position for an annual salary of $55,000. As agreed, I will start July 28, 20xx. Please let me know if I can do anything before then to facilitate the paperwork upon arrival.

Thank you and XYZ Company for expressing your confidence in me and my qualifications by offering me this position. I look forward to joining the XYZ marketing team and to contributing to its mission.

Sincerely,
Lane O'Brien

---

## TO REJECT:

As soon as you have definitely decided to reject a specific offer, as a common courtesy, immediately write your primary contact at that company a polite, concise note indicating that you have decided not to accept that company's offer. You do not have to provide a reason in your final rejection letter.

Many fortunate students receive multiple offers, ultimately accepting the one most favored. Upon accepting the chosen offer, and assuming no contingencies in the accepted offer, it is important to immediately write a polite rejection letter to the other companies that also made offers. Some students, in their understandable excitement over having just accepted an attractive position, delay or forget altogether to send rejection letters to other companies that made them offers. That is obviously inappropriate.

Here is an example of a rejection letter.

---

Robert Patterson
HR Director
ABC Corp.
Dear Mr. Patterson,

Thank you so much for offering me the Assistant Market Analyst position. After careful consideration, I have decided to decline your offer, having accepted another opportunity that seems more in line with my qualifications and career goals.

I enjoyed meeting you and the rest of your team. Thank you all very much for your time and energies in considering me as a potential member of your team at ABC.

Sincerely,
Wes Brinkley

# CAN YOU RENEGE?

❖ Definition of renege: "To fail to carry out a promise or commitment (e.g., reneged on the contract at the last minute)."

❖

❖ Most employment contracts and job offer letters include a phrase on "employment at will," which means that either party can terminate the agreement at any time and for any reason. Can you renege? Yes, if "employment at will" was in your signed offer.

❖

❖ Should you ever renege? *No!* A promise made is a promise to be kept. A promise broken, like a promise kept, is forever on your record. Employers, hiring managers, and recruiters talk with one another. Reneging is an ethical compromise on your part. Do you want that as part of your legacy?

❖

❖ Do not accept an offer if you are even thinking about reneging on it. If you feel you would renege on a would-be accepted offer from Company B if the dream job from Company A comes through, then ask for an extension from Company B, rather than accepting the offer. Refer back to the section on 'more than one offer' for additional perspectives and recommendations.

# WHAT IF A COMPANY RENEGES?[7]

As reviewed above, most employment contracts are employment at will, which means that either party can terminate the agreement at any time and for any reason. An employer pulling an offer prior to the start date would typically occur for one of two reasons. Your suggested recourse depends on which reason.

## Reason 1: It's on you.

Through screening you, the employer discovers a problem—e.g., failed drug tests, failed background check, false documentation in your resume.

Recourse: This is your problem. You could fight it, but you will have a low chance of successful resolution. Note, for example, the inclusion of the background check contingency in the offer letter example above.

# Reason 2: It's on them.

## A happy ending

A company change might lead to unexpected new financial constraints mandated from higher up in the company. Or, perhaps an unanticipated merger occurs after you accepted your offer. For example, an independent spirits distributor in Chicago merged with another distributor, totally eliminating the need for the new sales rep from a particular spirits supplier (Gallo, in this case). In the end, while the would-be new employee was obviously unsettled by this turn of events, the supplier came through with an alternative position for the new employee, albeit in a different city, but to the satisfaction of all parties.

## An unhappy ending

A company change causes an offer to be pulled after you accept it. What to do?

Try to make the best out of a bad situation. For example, when an offer is pulled due to unforeseen circumstances, you might have a chance to seek out an alternative position with this same company. To pursue this (admittedly non- optimal strategy) indicate that you were looking forward to joining the company and you understand that these things happen. Reiterate your qualifications and indicate your interest in potentially still landing that same position with this company later, once the air has cleared, or pursuing another opportunity with the company. Acting in such a professional, mature manner should position you well for future consideration from this company.

A more aggressive approach is having an employment attorney view your contract to see if the employer acted according to the agreement. Some contracts state that an employer must give you a specified amount of notice before terminating the contract, such as 30, 60, or 90 days. Others might stipulate that the company must pay you a certain financial compensation if the contract is ended.

Ask yourself, do I really want to start a conflicted conversation with the company? At a cost to me and without a full time position as a result? Probably not. In most such instances, it is best to chalk it up it up to bad experience and seek out an alternative position. Avoiding burning bridges in this manner will leave you with one or more strong advocates at the reneging firm. These advocates feel your pain and would be happy to recommend you for a similar position with other firms they have in their professional or personal networks.

## Step #6 REVIEW QUESTIONS

1. Under what circumstances should you accept the offer without negotiating?
2. Should you ever accept a verbal offer? Explain

3.  What if you receive an offer with a close in deadline, but are still waiting for another, more attractive offer, but have no idea whether or when that more attractive offer might materialize?

4.  How should you evaluate your offer? What should be in your offer?

5.  What questions should you ask about the offer itself?

6.  What questions should you ask about the company in general?

7.  Should you try to negotiate anything in your offer? If so, what should you try to negotiate? Salary? Any specific Benefits?

8.  When and how should you negotiate? What does it mean to 'Get' before you 'Give'?

9.  Can you renege on an offer you have accepted?

10. What to do if a company reneges on an offer made to you?

---

1 This section draws heavily from career.vt.edu/jobsearchguide/MultipleOffers.html

2 Input here from glassdoor.com/blog/negotiate-job-offer-part-1/

3 This section draws heavily from career.vt.edu/jobsearchguide/MultipleOffers.html

4 Most of the basics of these tips, with variations, come from careers.ucsc.edu/student/handouts/job%20offer-salary.pdf

5 careers.ucsc.edu/student/handouts/job%20offer-salary.pdf

6 cbsnews.com/media/the-15-most-affordable-places-to-live-in-america/16/

7 Most of the ideas here are from work.chron.com/employer-rescinds-job-offer-1164.html

# WRAP UP

The range of opportunities in marketing can be overwhelming for anyone trying to launch a successful marketing career. Finding and landing an attractive entry-level marketing position is particularly challenging for many.

We have offered a step-by-step process to help meet that challenge, including specific suggestions and detailed examples addressing:
- How to decide what type of entry level marketing position(s) best fits your interests and qualifications;
- How to prepare your materials for confidently and effectively pursuing your ideal entry-level position;
- How to find available entry-level marketing opportunities that match your interests;
- How to apply for specific available positions, once identified;
- How to effectively interview for those positions; and, finally,
- How to respond to offers, once received.

Our hope is that this step-by-step approach has helped to make your job search, application process, interviewing and offer evaluation as smooth and successful as possible.

Once you begin to live your marketing career, don't forget about the guidance offered in this book, as many of the strategies and tips provided can be used throughout your career as you strive to advance from one position to another.

We wish you the best in your quest for an interesting and satisfying entry-level position – one that will ultimately lead to a long, happy and successful dream marketing career.